Essays On Human Rights In India

Dr. Sushma Sharma

Copyright © 2016 Dr. Sushma Sharma

All rights reserved.

ISBN-10: **1523410426**
ISBN-13: **978-1523410422**

DEDICATION

I dedicate this book to my family.

CONTENTS

	Preface	vii
	Acknowledgments	ix
1	ECONOMIC EMPOWERMENT OF WOMEN	10
2	DOMESTIC VIOLENCE	18
3	SEXUAL AND REPRODUCTIVE RIGHTS OF INDIAN WOMEN	36
4	INTERNALLY DISPLACED PERSONS AND HUMAN RIGHTS	48
5	SEXUAL HARASSMENT OF WOMEN AT WORKPLACE	59
6	SEXUAL OFFENCE AGAINST WOMEN	71
7	HONOUR KILLING	80
8	CHILDREN AND HUMAN RIGHTS	93
9	RIGHT TO CLEAN ENVIRONMENT	114
10	RIGHT TO HEALTH	132
11	RIGHTS OF PRISONERS	144
12	ROLE OF NGOs as HUMAN RIGHTS DEFENDERS	159
13	BIBLIOGRAPHY	170
14	ABOUT THE AUTHOR	189
15	END-NOTES	190

Preface

Human rights are the basic and inalienable rights which are being conferred over all the human beings. There is no need to satisfy any qualification for enjoying these rights. Every human being is entitled to these rights only by the virtue of being born as a human being. These rights are the claims available to every human being irrespective of his colour, caste, creed, age, nationality, financial status, sex, educational qualification, region, religion etc. Primarily human rights can be classified into right to life, liberty, equality and dignity.

Unfortunately human rights violation is a common phenomenon in the present era. Violation of the human rights of women, children, prisoners, disabled people, elderly, internally and externally displaced people, labourers etc is a bitter reality in almost all the regions, Nations and societies across the world. Most of the victims belong to vulnerable groups, they are often unaware of their human rights and even if they are aware they don't have any protection against such kind of abuses. The machinery of State is either incompetent to deal with such violations or is poorly equipped or in most of the cases the execution of laws is so sluggish that it defeats the ends of justice.

India is the seventh largest country in territory and the second largest in terms the population in the world. Dozens of religious beliefs are followed and hundreds of languages are spoken here. It is not easy to maintain the human right norms in such a vast and diversified society. India is a member of the United Nations, and also a signatory of almost all the important conventions and treaties related to the protection, promotion and preservation of human rights. Still it is not easy to ensure observation of all the human rights norms .This book is intended primarily to address few selected areas of human rights jurisprudence and analysis of those areas in shape of essays. It is aims to fulfill the needs of law students at the graduate and post graduate levels, though it is also intended to be a useful text for anyone interested in knowing about human rights.

I have tried to highlight some of these issues in my book. Though this book reflects my efforts it is also including the compilation of the ideas of many great authors on the subject. I acknowledge to have taken some portions of this book from the literature provided in the bibliography, other authorities and web-sites.

I am aware that human rights law is vast and is enriched by national and international developments; the new human right norms are being added and new areas are covered with in its scope every year, judicial pronouncements are also shaping and enriching it day by day. Moreover I have limited the book to only a few topics. Because of this reason my book requires constant up-dating. I would sincerely welcome the guidance and suggestions all the readers for improving this book in future.

2016   **Dr. Sushma Sharma**

ACKNOWLEDGMENTS

This book could not have been realized without the help of a large number of people. Although it is not possible to acknowledge each of them in true sense, for their crucial and valuable support, the following are the people who made this book possible.

Prof. Dr. S.S. Singh, Director of The National Law Institute University, Bhopal has provided constant encouragement and gave valuable suggestions for improving this book.

The library staff of The National Law Institute University deserves special thanks for their help. I also thank the publisher and printer who are extremely co operative with all the short notice schedules.

I extend my thanks to Mrs. Susheela Sharma, my respected mother in law, my husband Mr. Prashant Kumar Sharma and my dear children Adi and Jai (Honey) for their quite support and constant encouragement.

I extend my gratitude to my loving parents Dr. S.P. Mistry and Mrs. Shanti Devi and to my brother Mr. Subhash Mistry for their blessings and encouragement. I offer a special thanks to my younger brother Er. Heeresh Mistry, without whose vital help the book would not have been turned into a reality.

I also thank almighty god and all my respected teachers for granting their blessings and wisdom.

Dr. Sushma Sharma

Essay –I

ECONOMIC EMPOWERMENT OF WOMEN

Introduction

All men and women are born free and equal in dignity and rights. Famous Jurist Roscoe Pound once emphasised upon the concept of 'balancing of interests' in his theory known as Social Engineering Theory. Pound had insisted that, "the structure of public, social and individual interests are all, in fact, individual interests looked at from different points of view for the purpose of clarity and therefore, in order to make the system work properly, it is essential that when interests are balanced, all claims must be translated into the same level and carefully labelled."This analogy involves the concept of equality between the men and women.

Economic empowerment is the key for self respect and freedom and women are equally capable to undertake any kind of employment as efficiently as men. Lord Denning has observed in his book *Due Process of Law*, that a women feels as keenly thinks as clearly, as a man. She in her sphere does work as useful as man does in his. She has as much right to her freedom-develop her personality to the full-as a man. When she marries, she does not become the husband's servant but his equal partner. If his work is more important in life of the community, her's is more important in the life of the family. Neither can do without the other. Neither is above the other or under the other. They are equals.

The U.N. Secretary General, Kofi Annan, had stated once, "Gender equality is more than a goal in itself. It is a precondition for meeting the challenge of reducing poverty, promoting sustainable development and building good governance." The women who does not work outside the home are definitely not *"non- workers"* as their labour could also be converted into money but their labour is not recognised in the male dominated Indian patriarchal system. Women in employment not only develops her independence and personality but she also becomes an asset to her family and the society. Thus the economically empowered women is able to contribute in a better manner towards the development of the society and the Country as a whole. Gender equality in the sphere of employment builds an amicable and safe environment for women to work at ease and to give the benefit of her qualities to the society.

Robert Ingersoll, had also commented once that, "There will never be a generation of great men until there has been a generation of free women-of free mind".

According to The Centre for Enquiry into Health and Allied Themes (CEHAT), in India" social norms and cultural practices are deep rooted in a highly patriarchal social order where women are expected to adhere to strict gender roles about what they can and cannot do. Women are subject to double discrimination, being members of a specific caste, class or ethnic group, apart from experiencing gendered vulnerabilities. Women in Indian society have low status as compared to men. They have little control on the resources and on important decisions related to their lives.

The combination of Constitutional Principles, Statutes and International Conventions are used in the jurisprudence of economic empowerment of women as a tool to recognise, protect and preserve their rights in the male dominated society of India. Along with the efforts of Legislators and executive the role of the Apex court is no less important. In fact the judicial creativity has paved way for the effective realization of the Constitutional and statutory rights of Indian women.

International Perspective

At this juncture, we may refer to some international conventions and treaties on gender equality. The Covenant on the Elimination of All Forms of Discrimination Against Women (CEDAW), 1979, is the United Nations' landmark treaty marking the struggle for women's right. It is regarded as the Bill of Rights for women. It graphically puts what constitutes discrimination against women and spells out tools so that women's rights are not violated and they are conferred the same rights.

The equality principles were reaffirmed in the Second World Conference on Human Rights at Vienna in June 1993 and in the Fourth World Conference on Women held in Beijing in 1995. India was a party to this Convention and other Declarations and is committed to actualize them. In 1993 Conference, gender-based violence and all categories of sexual harassment and exploitation were condemned. A part of the Resolution reads thus:

The human rights of women and of the girl child are an inalienable, integral and indivisible part of universal human rights. The World Conference on Human Rights urges governments, institutions, intergovernmental and non-governmental organizations to intensify their efforts for the protection of human rights of women and the girl child.

The other relevant International Instruments on Women are: (i) Universal Declaration of Human Rights (1948), (ii) Convention on the Political Rights of Women (1952), (iii) International Covenant on Civil and Political Rights (1966), (iv) International Covenant on Economic, Social and Cultural Rights (1966), (v) Declaration on the Elimination of All Forms of Discrimination against Women (1967), (vi) Declaration on the Protection of Women and Children in Emergency and Armed Conflict (1974), (vii) Inter-American Convention for the Prevention, Punishment and Elimination of Violence against Women (1995), (viii) Universal Declaration on Democracy (1997), and (ix) Optional Protocol to the Convention on the Elimination of All Forms of Discrimination against Women (1999).

Convention for Elimination of all forms of Discrimination Against Women (for short, "CEDAW") was ratified by the UNO on 18-12-1979 and the Government of India had ratified as an active participant on 19-6-1993 acceded to CEDAW and reiterated that discrimination against women violates the principles of equality of rights and respect for human dignity and it is an obstacle to the participation on equal terms with men in the political, social, economic and cultural life of their country; it hampers the growth of the personality from society and family, making more difficult for the full development of potentialities of women in the service of the respective countries and of humanity.[i]

Human Rights of Women and the Constitution of India

The Constitution of India is true guarantor of right of equality of women. It is a fundamental document which deals with women's right to Equality in India. Which is the first condition of economic empowerment. Further the Constitution of India provide special protection to women with the help of various provisions inserted under Part III. Besides, the constitutional framework Indian Parliament has also framed various legislations to protect women's rights.

The Constitution of India adopted in 1950 provides certain rights to its citizens known as the Fundamental Rights (Part-3, Article 14-35). Supreme Court has held that provisions of part III of the Constitution of India should be given widest possible interpretation. Article 14 guarantees equality before law and the equal protection of law. Article 15 prohibits discrimination on any basis. It also deals with the special provisions to be made for women which shall not be considered as discriminatory. Article 16 provides equal opportunity in matters of public employment. Part IV of the Constitution of India deals with Directive Principles of State Policy. Article 39[ii] in Part IV of the Constitution that deals with Directive Principles of State Policy, provides that the State shall direct its policies towards securing that the citizens, men and women equally, have the right to adequate means of livelihood. Clause (d) of the said Article provides for equal pay for equal work for both men and women and Clause (e) stipulates that health and strength of workers, men and women, and the tender age of children are not abused and that citizens are not forced by economic necessity to enter into avocations unsuited to their age or strength.

Article 42 imposes an obligation on the State to make provision for securing just and humane conditions of work and for maternity relief.

In *Minerva Milts Ltd. v. Union of India* [iii], the Constitution Bench has found that the Fundamental Rights and the Directive Principles are the two quilts of the chariot in establishing the egalitarian social order. In *Society for Unaided Private Schools of Rajasthan v. Union of India and Anr.* [iv], it has been held that the Court is required to interpret the Fundamental Rights in the light of the Directive Principles.

The 73rd and 74th Constitutional Amendment Acts are new dimensions in the advancement of women in India. Reservation of seats for women in Panchayats and Municipalities have been provided Under Articles 243(d) and 243(t) of the Constitution of India. The purpose of the constitutional amendment is that the women in India are required to participate more in a democratic set-up especially at the grass root level. This is an affirmative step in the realm of women empowerment. The 73rd and 74th amendment of the Constitution which deals with the reservation of women has the avowed purpose, that is, the women should become parties in the decision making process in a democracy that is governed by rule of law. Their active participation in the decision making process has been accentuated upon and the secondary rule which was historically given to women has been sought to be metamorphosed to the primary one. In spite of all these provisions women in India are victims of personal laws which restrict them from representation in the society.

The Article 51-A.(Fundamental Duties) Clauses (e) and (j) and provide as follows:

(e) to promote harmony and the spirit of common brotherhood amongst all the people of India transcending religious, linguistic and regional or sectional diversities; to renounce practices derogatory to the dignity of women;

practices derogatory to the dignity of women are to be renounced. Be it stated, dignity is the quintessential quality of a personality and a human frames always desires to live in the mansion of dignity, for it is a highly cherished value. Clause (j) has to be understood in the backdrop that India is a welfare State and, therefore, it is the duty of the State to promote justice, to provide equal opportunity to see that all citizens and they are not deprived of by reasons of economic disparity. It is also the duty of the State to frame policies so that men and women have the right to adequate means of livelihood. It is also the duty of the citizen to strive towards excellence in all spheres of individual and collective activity so that the nation constantly rises to higher levels of endeavour and achievement.

Judicial Response

The public at large have faith in our Judiciary. The Supreme Court is the final interpreter of the Constitution of India. The judiciary is the protector of Human Rights over decades. The initiative of Judiciary has been shown in its various verdicts. The Supreme Court of India has interpreted various provisions of international instruments correlated with Constitutional law of India. India is a signatory to various International Conventions and Treaties. The Universal Declaration of Human Rights adopted on 10th Dec. 1948, has greatly helped to create a universal thinking that Human Rights are supreme shall preserve. *In Madhu Kishwar v. State*, Supreme Court has considered the provisions of the Convention on the Elimination of All Forms of Discrimination against Women, 1979 and held that it is a mirror image of Part III and Part IV of the Constitution of India. The Supreme Court of India had admitted that provisions of international instruments are not in conflict with National Laws.

In *Valsamma Paul (Mrs) v. Cochin University*[v] The Supreme Court has observed that the Human rights are derived from the dignity and worth inherent in the human person. Human rights and fundamental freedoms have been reiterated in the Universal Declaration of Human Rights. Democracy, development and respect for human rights and fundamental freedoms are interdependent and have mutual reinforcement. The human rights for women, including girl child are, therefore, inalienable, integral and an indivisible part of universal human rights. The full development of personality and fundamental freedoms and equal participation by women in political, social, economic and cultural life are concomitants for national development, social and family stability and growth--cultural, social and economical. All forms of discrimination on grounds of gender is violative of fundamental freedoms and human rights... On a perusal of the Articles of the aforesaid Convention(CEDAW), it is clear as crystal that apart from right to work being an inalienable right of all human beings, it has commended the right to same employment opportunity, including the application of same criteria for selection in matters of employment and all steps to be taken to eliminate discrimination against women in the field of employment in order to ensure equality among man and women. It is founded on social security and many other facets.

In *Madhu Kishwar* v. *State of Bihar*[vi] this Court had stated that Indian women have suffered and are suffering discrimination in silence ...Self-sacrifice and self-denial are their nobility and fortitude and yet they have been subjected to all inequities, indignities, inequality and discrimination."[vii]

In *Voluntary Health Assn. of Punjab v. Union of India*[viii], it has been observed that it would not be an exaggeration to say that a society that does not respect its women cannot be treated to be civilised.

In *Mrs. Neera Mathur v. Life Insurance Corporation of India and Anr.*[ix], a female candidate was required to furnish information about her menstrual period, last date of menstruation, pregnancy and miscarriage. The Court declared that calling of such information are indeed embarrassing if not humiliating. The Court directed that the employer i.e. Life Insurance Corporation would do well to delete such columns in the declaration. In *Maya Devi*[x], the requirement that a married women should obtain her husband's consent before applying for public employment was held invalid and unconstitutional. The Court observed that such a requirement is an anachronistic obstacle to women's equality.

In *Mackinnon Mackenzie and Co. Ltd. v. Audrey D'Costa*[xi], the Court was deliberating the issue of equal pay for equal work in the context of female stenographers and male stenographers. Dealing with the aspect of discrimination, the Court opined:

It may be that the management was not employing any male as a Confidential Stenographer attached to the senior executives in its establishment and that there was no transfer of Confidential Lady Stenographers to the general pool of Stenographers where males were working. It, however, ought not to make any difference for purposes of the application of the Act when once it is established that the lady Stenographers were doing practically the same kind of work which the male Stenographers were discharging. The employer is bound to pay the same remuneration to both of them irrespective of the place where they were working unless it is shown that the women are not fit to do the work of the male Stenographers. Nor can the management deliberately create such conditions of work only with the object of driving away women from a particular type of work which they can otherwise perform with the object of paying them less remuneration elsewhere in its establishment.

In *Vishakha v. State of Rajasthan* [xii] case. The Court referred to the 1993 Treaty and opined that the meaning and content of Fundamental Rights in the Constitution are of sufficient amplitude to encompass all the facets of gender equality including prevention of sexual harassment or abuse. In that context, the Court observed thus:

"The international conventions and norms are to be read into them in the absence of enacted domestic law occupying the fields when there is no inconsistency between them. It is now an accepted rule of judicial construction that regard must be had to international conventions and norms fro construing domestic law when there is no inconsistency between them and there is a void in the domestic law.

The three-Judge Bench, while noting the increasing awareness on gender justice, took note of the increase in the effort to guard against such violations. The Court observed that when there is violation of gender justice and working women is sexually harassed, there is violation of the fundamental rights of gender justice and it is clear violation of the rights Under Articles 14, 15 and 21 of the Constitution.

In *Municipal Corporation of Delhi v. Female Workers (Muster Roll)*,[xiii] the court decided the question of non-grant of maternity leave to the non regular female workers on muster roll. The S.C. decided the case in their favour and held that A just social order can be achieved only when inequalities are obliterated and everyone is provided what, is legally due. When who constitute almost half of the segment of our society have to be honoured and treated with dignity at places where they work to earn their livelihood. Whatever be the nature of their duties, their avocation and the place where they work; they must be provided all the facilities to which they are entitled. To become a mother is the most natural phenomena in the life of a woman. Whatever is needed to facilitate the birth of child to a woman who is in service, the employer has to be considerate and sympathetic towards her and must realise the physical difficulties which a working woman would face in performing her duties at the work place while carrying a baby in the womb or while rearing up the child after birth. The Maternity Benefit Act, 1961 aims to provide all these facilities to a working woman in a dignified manner so that she may overcome the state of motherhood honourably, peaceably, undeterred by the fear, of being victimised for forced absence during the pre or post-natal period.

In the case of *Charu Khurana v. Union of India*[xiv] a writ petition preferred under Article 32 of the Constitution of India,which according to J.Deepak Misra, exposes with luminosity the prevalence of gender inequality in the film industry, which compels one to contemplate whether the fundamental conception of gender empowerment and gender justice have been actualised despite number of legislations and progressive outlook in society or behind the liberal exterior, there is a facade which gets uncurtained on apposite discernment.

S.C. has held that, The Cine Costume Make-up Artists and Hair Dressers Association has been making a distinction between the male and female by categorising them as make-up artists and hair dressers respectively, as a result of which, the women, who are eligible and qualified to become make-up artist, never become make-up artist and only function as hair dressers. The learned Counsel would also contend that the women have been harassed at the workplace whenever they get an engagement as a make-up artist.

Thus, the aforesaid decision unequivocally recognises gender equality as a fundamental right. The discrimination done by the Association, a trade union registered under the Act, whose rules have been accepted, cannot take the route of the discrimination solely on the basis of sex. It really plays foul of the statutory provisions. It is absolutely violative of constitutional values and norms. If a female artist does not get an opportunity to enter into the arena of being a member of the Association, she cannot work as a female artist. It is inconceivable. The likes of the Petitioners are given membership as hair dressers, but not as make-up artist. There is no fathomable reason for the same. It is gender bias writ large. It is totally impermissible and wholly unacceptable.

The analysis of these case laws indicates that the judiciary has tried to give a wider meaning to the Constitutional provisions so that women could be economically empowered. The Supreme Court has read the essence of the legal provisions and the Constitutional provisions for ensuring the right of employment of women. Even in the areas where there is legislative vacuum the courts have filled in the gap if the legislations to provide relief. The law has been interpreted by the Courts for the purpose of applying it in the changed social scenario. In this manner the Supreme Court has tried to develop the law to promote economic empowerment of women in the light of newly emerging problems.

Essay-II

DOMESTIC VIOLENCE

Introduction

Domestic Violence might be a new technical term but the phenomenon of domestic violence is not new for any Indian women. It is a common bitter reality in the lives of majority of women irrespective of their, educational or financial status, caste, creed, beauty, profession etc. Women are often subjected to domestic violence at the hands of their in husband and in laws. The reason behind domestic violence might range from demand from dowry to simply inferiority complex. One of the reasons for domestic violence being so prevalent is the orthodox and idiotic mindset of the society that women are physically and emotionally weaker than the males.

To understand the essence of the word domestic violence first of all we should know the meaning of the words domestic and violence separately. The word domestic means "within the realm or the territory of house". [xv] And the word violence means "action using physical force and intended to hurt or kill someone to cause damage".[xvi] Thus the word domestic violence means "an action or physical force which is being used within the realm or territory of house with an intention to hurt or cause damage any particular subject in the domestic household".

The term used to describe this exploding problem of violence within our homes is Domestic Violence. This violence is towards someone who we are in a relationship with, be it a wife, husband, son, daughter, mother, father, grandparent or any other family member. It can be a male's or a female's atrocities towards another male or a female. Anyone can be a victim and a victimizer. This violence has a tendency to explode in various forms such as physical, sexual or emotional.[xvii]

According to United Nation Population Fund Report, around two-third of married Indian women are victims of domestic violence and as many as 70 per cent of married women in India between the age of 15 and 49 are victims of beating, rape or forced sex. In India, more than 55 percent of the women suffer from domestic violence, especially in the states of Bihar, U.P., M.P. and other northern states.[xviii]

In general sense, domestic violence is violence that occurs within the private sphere, generally between individuals who are related through intimacy, blood or law. Despite the apparent neutrality of the term, domestic violence is nearly always a gender-specific crime, perpetrated by men against women. Thus any domestic violence law should ideally put a stop to violence, give protection against future abuse and use punitive measures to combat continued domestic violence.[xix]

Domestic violence, also known as domestic abuse, spousal abuse, battering, family violence, dating abuse, and intimate partner violence (IPV), is a pattern of behavior which involves the abuse by one partner against another in an intimate relationship such as marriage, cohabitation, dating or within the family.
 In spite of the extreme physical and psychological violence meted out on many women, they do not seek divorce, as they feel their trauma and that of their children is too great a price to be paid instead. Thus to a great extent she accepts domestic violence as part of her family life.[xx]

 It is a violence which takes place within the realm or territory of house; it is palpable that the victims of such violence will be the family members. That is why it is to be said that "domestic violence is an abuse which manifests itself when a spouse or a family member violates another physically or psychologically"[xxi].

Domestic Violence can take place between husband and wife, child and parent, people of same sex as well as the people of different sex.[xxii] Overall it can be said to be a preliminary stage of a crime of power and abuse.[xxiii] It is a behavior of usually an individual who is in the position to dominate the victim due to seniority by age, relation, financial status, education or simply because the victim is timid and having submissive and soft nature. The purpose is to maintain coercive control over the other.

Types

Domestic violence could be of either category physical or mental. Physical forms would include female foeticide, selective abortion, dowry harassment, dowry deaths, physical abuse like beating battering, not giving food and causing starvation and all other kinds of cruelties. Mental violence includes mental torture, abuses, calling names, commenting about physical features, like she is not beautiful or not well cultured, social humiliation etc. It includes all kinds of threat of abuse of physical, sexual, verbal, emotional and economical nature that can harm or cause injury to the health, safety to life, limb or well being, either mental or physical of the aggrieved person.[xxiv]

The word physical means "Something related to body rather than mind or relating to things that you can see hear or feel".[xxv] It is the intentional use of physical force with the potential of causing bodily injury, harm, disability, or death.

Women may be affected in a number of ways. They may experience any or all of the following: Loss of opportunity; isolation from family/friends; loss of income or work; homelessness; emotional/psychological effects such as experiences of anxiety, depression or lowered sense of self-worth; poor health; physical injury or ongoing impairment; if they are pregnant they may miscarry or the baby may be stillborn; time of work or study, and long-term impact on financial security and career; death (two women a week are killed by their partners or former partners). Battered women have tendency to remain quiet, agonized and emotionally disturbed after the occurrence of the torment. A psychological set back and trauma because of domestic violence affects women's productivity in all forms of life. The suicide case of such victimized women is also a deadly consequence and the number of such cases is increasing.[xxvi]

The Protection of Women from Domestic Violence Act, 2005 defines sexual abuse as, "Any act or conduct which is of such a nature so as to cause bodily pain, harm, or danger to life, limb or health or compare the health or development of the aggrieved person and includes assault, criminal intimidation and criminal force". Physical acts such as hitting, slapping, pushing, pulling, causing alarm, kicking, threatening to harm constitutes physical abuse.

Violence which affects the human mind is called emotional violence. It is the deliberate act of doing something to make the victim feel diminished or embarrassed or isolated. This type of abuse is the hardest to spot because the injury is not physical or immediately visible. People undergoing emotional abuse are often seen to suffer from depression which puts them at an increasing risk of suicide, eating disorders, drug and alcohol abuse. The victims of emotional abuse are often accused to be oversensitive. There are various degrees of it and it is also very difficult to prove emotional abuse.

Economical or financial abuse

Here, money is used as the means of having control over the partner. Thus we can say that, "when the abuser has complete control of the victim's money and other economic resources, is called economic abuse".[xxvii] For example, if a person is earning for the fulfillment of his or her necessities but he is not free to spend his or her money according to their interest, there is another person commanding the expenditures, it is called economic violence. It may also happen when the victim is fully dependent for her maintenance on the husband and the husband deprives her of the necessities. No money is provided or sufficient amount is not paid on demand to the victim. Thus victim is unable to fulfill her requirements. Sometimes this may also happen that the victim is a working women and she is stopped from working so that she will lose her financial independence. On the contrary in some cases a women who would prefer to be at home is compelled to go out and earn money , both the categories comprise of tortures.

Section 5 clause (iv) of Protection of women from domestic Violence Act discusses economic abuse as deprivation of all or any economic or financial resources to which the aggrieved person is entitled under any law or custom whether payable under an order of a court or otherwise or which the aggrieved person requires out of necessity including, but not limited to, household necessities for the aggrieved person and her children, if any, stridhan, property, jointly or separately owned by the aggrieved person, payment of rental related to the shared household and maintenance;

Sexual Violence

Sexual violence is a combination of physical and mental torture. It is any assault or unwanted act of a sexual nature. "It can include anything from exhibitionism and exposures to pornography to unwanted sexual touching, to rape, to injuring or endangering the life or the victim".[xxviii] Section (3) clause (ii) of Protection of women from Domestic violence act deals with sexual abuse as it includes any conduct of a sexual nature that abuses humanity, degrades or otherwise violates the dignity of women".[xxix]

Verbal abuse

Verbal abuse is giving its meaning itself as such type of abuse which hurts somebody verbally or that violence which is committed by the words either written or spoken. It is also called as revealing is a form of abusive behavior involving the use of language. "It is a form of profanity in that it can occur with or without the use of expletives". [xxx] Verbal abuse is somewhat is responsible to create emotional or psychological abuse, because if somebody verbally abuse to another then he got hurt and he started thinking and which creates psychological abuse. Verbal abuse my result from use of filthy and insulting language, talking rudely, comparison of the victim with persons of lower character ,imputation of committing illegal or immoral activities, singing dirty ballads, using slangs for the victim or insulting in any other way by saying bad things about the victim or her relatives or friends. The Protection of women from Domestic Violence act 2005 deals verbal and emotional abuse along with in section 3 clause (iii) of this act stated that, "verbal and emotional abuse includes- insults, ridicule, humiliation, name calling and insults or ridicule specially with regard to not having a child or a male child; and repeated threats to cause physical pain to any person in whom the aggrieved person is interested.[xxxi]

Perpetrators of domestic violence

Perpetrator of domestic violence can be anyone between 17- 80 years and can be of any sex, socioeconomic, racial, ethnic, occupational, educational, and religious group. Perpetrators are not always angry and hostile. Some of them might be suffering from psychiatric problems, such as depression, post - traumatic stress disorder, or psychopathology but all abusers are not mentally ill. Abusers differ in patterns of abuse and levels of dangerousness. While there is not an agreed upon universal psychological profile, perpetrators do share a behavioral profile that is described as "an ongoing pattern of coercive control involving various forms of intimidation, and psychological and physical abuse." Perpetrators of domestic violence need not be men only. It can be women as well when violence is perpetrated by women in the family by mother, mother–in-law, sister-in-law, sisters, etc.

Domestic violence is sadly a reality in Indian society, a truism. In the Indian patriarchal setup, it became an acceptable practice to abuse women. There may be many reasons for the occurrence of domestic violence. From a feminist standpoint, it could be said that the occurrence of domestic violence against women arises out of the patriarchal setup, the stereotyping of gender roles and the distribution of power real or perceived, in society. Following such ideology, men are believed to be stronger than women and more powerful. They control women and their lives and as a result of this power play, they may hurt women with impunity. The role of the woman is to accept her 'fate' and the violence employed against her meekly.[xxxii]

Gender equity and social development are inseparably interlinked. In addition to the above criteria another important criterion required to be able to create gender equity would be to do away with the fact of violence against women in particular with domestic violence which is widely prevalent in India but which unlike most other forms of violence against women is scarcely acknowledged as being widespread and is hardly ever treated as a crime. Instead, Indian society makes domestic violence invisible. Domestic violence is one of the few phenomena which cut across all the cultural, socio-economic, educational, ethnic and religious barriers. This type of violence not only seems to increase even with rise in women's education but also prevails among the elite sections of the society. Violence by intimate family members is one of South Asia's darkest legacies. In a survey on violence against women in India, 94 percent of the cases involved an offender who was a member of the family.[xxxiii]

India needs to develop a comprehensive domestic violence policy so that at least, the institutional response to the issue will give the battered women a choice whether or not they choose to remain in relationship with someone who has perpetrated domestic violence and access to aid in the form of health-care, childcare and shelter. The response to recognize that there are many forms of domestic violence--not restricted to life-threatening situations but also including emotional, physical, sexual, psychological and financial abuse--and it consequently should be flexible enough to be able to deal with the whole spectrum of violence.[xxxiv]

International Developments
After successfully pushing for the inclusion of a commitment to equal rights for women in the UN Charter and Universal Declaration of Human Rights, women's organizations worked for the establishment of the UN Commission on the Status of Women and other formal mechanisms for the advancement of women's status. The Commission and affiliated nongovernmental organizations (NGOs) drafted a variety of conventions to combat discrimination against women internationally and pressed for the General Assembly to declare a Decade for Women program. It was the international

resurgence of women's activism in the 1960s and 1970s, and the pressure generated by women's organizations internationally, that made the UN Decade for Women (1975-1985) a reality. As the Decade unfolded, women's rights activists coordinated international efforts to study the position of women in all societies and the reasons for their subordinate status.

The main provisions of Convention on the Elimination of All Forms of Discrimination against Women, 1979 that are applicable to cases of Domestic Violence are as follows. Article 2 declares comprehensive state obligation to eliminate discrimination against women. Article 5 defines Elimination of prejudices and practices, based on the stereotyped roles of women and men. Article 16 protected women from elimination of discrimination in marriage and family relations: equality of women and men, same rights and responsibility.

Article 253 of the Constitution confers on the Parliament the power to make laws in pursuance of international treaties, conventions, etc. The Domestic Violence Act was passed in furtherance of the recommendations of the United Nations Committee on the CEDAW. Article 2 of the Declaration on the Elimination of Violence against Women, identifies three areas in which violence commonly takes place. They are a) violence occurring within the family b) violence occurring in the general community and c) violence perpetrated or condoned by the state.

In 1985, the participants at the Final Conference of the Decade for Women in Nairobi, Kenya, reached a consensus that violence against women exists in various forms in everyday life in all societies. Women are beaten, mutilated, burned, sexually abused and raped. Such violence is a major obstacle to the achievement of peace and other objectives of the Decade and should be given special attention. National machinery should be established in order to deal with the question of violence against women within the family and society. [xxxv]

In 1989, the UN Commission on the Status of Women in Vienna compiled a mass of domestic violence statistics and analyses by women's rights activists and academics, and published its report, Violence against Women in the Family. The report's author reviewed over 250 articles, books, and studies of various aspects of domestic violence, of which only ten had been published earlier than 1971. Furthermore, the report is only a small sample of the huge amount of new material being published about this old problem.[xxxvi]

In 1992, during the 11th session of the CEDAW committee, the United Nations issued General Recommendation Number 19, which pertains specifically to the issue of violence against women. Although the provisions of this recommendation are not legally binding, as a signatory to CEDAW, India has a general obligation to take cognizance of these recommendations.[xxxvii]

The General Recommendation No. 19 can be of particular importance in cases of domestic violence, as it clarifies:

"Traditional attitudes by which women are regarded as subordinate to men or as having stereotyped roles perpetuate widespread practices involving violence or coercion, such as family violence and abuse, forced marriage, dowry deaths….(etc). Such prejudices and practices may justify gender-based violence as a form of protection or control of women. The effect of such violence on the physical and mental integrity of women is to deprive them the equal enjoyment, exercise and knowledge of human rights and fundamental freedoms."

The Declaration on the Elimination of Violence Against Women, adopted by the UN General Assembly in 1993, defines Violence Against women as "any act of gender-based violence that results in, or is likely to result in, physical, sexual or psychological harm, or suffering to women including threats of such acts, coercion or arbitrary deprivation of liberty; whether occurring in public or private life"

The preamble of the Vienna Declaration and Program of Action, 1993 emphasizes that every human person is the central subject of human rights, and upholds the notion of human rights for all without distinction based on sex. Article 18 declares human rights for women as being indivisible with universal human rights, and stated that the international community should prioritize the eradication of all forms of discrimination based on sex. The declaration also points out that gender-based violence resulting from cultural prejudice harms human dignity, and should be eliminated through legal measures and national action. Article 36, 37, 38, 39, 40, 41, 42, 43, 44 reaffirms the equal status and human rights of women. For international community to implement elimination of all forms of discrimination against women, Article 83 urges Government to take national action, and integrate standards into domestic legislation and social system.[xxxviii]

Beijing Declaration and Platform for Action was adopted by consensus in 1995, at the Fourth World Conference on Women. The Fourth World Conference on Women was noteworthy because it drew considerable attention to the severity of the issue of violence against women

Constitutional provisions

The preamble to the Indian constitution contains various goals including "the equality of status and opportunity" to all citizens. It has been the basis for legislation like Modern Hindu Law which aim at giving equal status and right of women.

Article 14 contains the equal protection clause. It affirms equality before the law and the equal protection of the laws. Article 14 prohibits class legislation, but permits classification for legislative purposes. A law does not become unconstitutional simply because it applies to one set of persons and not another. Where a law effects a classification and is challenged as being violative of this Article, the law may be declared valid if it satisfies the following two conditions:

1. The classification must be based on some intelligible differentia,

2. There must be a rational nexus between this differentia and the object sought to be achieved by the law.

Article 15 disallows discrimination on the grounds of religion, caste, sex, race, etc., but permits the State to make special provisions for certain classes of persons, including women and children. Article 15(3) empower the state to make special laws with a positive act where giving preferential treatment in favour of women.

Article 16 provides for equality of opportunity for all citizens in matters relating to employment or appointment to any office under the State.

All these are fundamental rights. Therefore, a woman can go to the court if one is subjected to any discrimination.

Criminal law
Section 113(A) and (B) of the Indian Evidence Act; Section 498(A) and 304(B) of the Indian Penal Code deals with domestic violence. Indian Penal Code , Section 498A, IPC, explains: Whoever, being the husband or the relative of the husband of a woman, subjects such woman to cruelty shall be punished with imprisonment for a term which may extend to three years and shall also be liable to fine. This sec deals with four types of cruelty:

Any conduct that is likely to drive a woman to suicide,

Any conduct which is likely to cause grave injury to the life, limb or health of the woman,

Harassment with the purpose of forcing the woman or her relatives to give some property,

Harassment because the woman or her relatives are either unable to yield to the demand for more money or do not give some share of the property.

Section 498A of the Indian Penal Code, is a criminal offence. It is a cognizable, non-bail able, and non compoundable offence.

Section 113(a), Indian Evidence Act says, "Where a married woman commits suicide within 7 years of her married life and it is shown that her husband or his relatives had treated her with cruelty, it would be presumed by the Court that her husband or relatives had aided (abetted) her suicide". Section 113(b) of Indian Evidence Act states that, "Presumption as to dowry death.- When the question is whether a person has committed the dowry death of a woman and it is shown that soon before her death such woman had been subjected by such person to cruelty or harassment for, or in connection with, any demand for dowry, the court shall presume that such person had caused the dowry death."

Section 304(b) of IPC says, "(1) Where the death of a woman is caused by any burns or bodily injury or occurs otherwise than under normal circumstances within seven years of her marriage and it is shown that soon before her death she was subjected to cruelty or harassment by her husband or by any relative of her husband, or in connection with, any demand for dowry, such death shall be called "dowry death" and such husband or relative shall be deemed to have caused her death. For the purpose of this sub-section, "dowry" shall have the same meaning as in section 2 of the Dowry Prohibition Act, 1961 (28 of 1961). (2) Whoever commits dowry death shall be punished with imprisonment for a term which shall not be less than seven years but which may extend to imprisonment for life."

The Protection of Women from Domestic Violence Act, 2005
An important advance made by the Act in understanding the nature of domestic violence has been in the combination of civil and criminal remedies. While civil remedies can be tailored to meet the circumstances of each case, criminal sanctions provide a greater deterrent effect among perpetrators.

The preamble to this Act reads like a definition and covers the entire subject matter of the Act. Apart from stating that the Act is intended to effectively protect the rights of a women and to give them a decent and dignified status, it stresses on the need of an 'aggrieved women' to seek immediate relief, compensation and also rehabilitation.

This Act contains 5 chapters and 37 sections. Its main features are firstly that the term 'domestic violence' has been made wide enough to encompass every possibility as it covers all forms of physical, sexual, verbal, emotional and economic abuse that can harm, cause injury to, endanger the health, safety, life, limb or well-being, either mental or physical of the aggrieved person. This is a genuinely wide definition and covers every eventuality. Secondly, the definition of an 'aggrieved' person' is equally wide and covers not just the wife but a woman who is the sexual partner of the male irrespective of whether she is his legal wife or not. The daughter, mother, sister, child (male or female), widowed relative, in fact, any woman residing in the household who is related in some way to the respondent, is also covered by the Act. The respondent under the definition given in the Act is "any male, adult person who is, or has been, in a domestic relationship with the aggrieved person" but so that his mother, sister and other relatives do not go scot free, the case can also be filed against relatives of the husband or male partner.[xxxix]

The Protection of Women from Domestic Violence Act, 2005 says that any act, conduct, omission or commission that harms or injures or has the potential to harm or injure will be considered domestic violence by the law. Even a single act of omission or commission may constitute domestic violence - in other words, women do not have to suffer a prolonged period of abuse before taking recourse to law. The law covers children also.

Information can be given to protection officer by any person who has reason to believe that an act of domestic violence has been, or is being or is likely to be committed.[xl]

There has been an effort in this Act to simplify and make more effective issues of the method of filing a complaint of domestic violence for obtaining relief. It also simplifies procedural matters for an aggrieved who wishes to file a complaint. For example, the Act allows anyone, perhaps a friend or an NGO that has witnessed a case of domestic violence, to file a complaint in that regard to the Protection Officer.

Scope of The Protection Of Women From Domestic Violence Act 2005:-

It is a central acts extending to the whole of India expect Jammu & Kashmir. It came into force on 26th October 2006.The offences under this act are cognizable and non-bailable. The Act covers those women who are in relationship with the abuser or where both parties have lived together by consanguinity or by marriage, are entitled to legal protection under this Act.

It provides for the appointment of protection officer who can provide the aggrieved person with legal aid, medical examination and safe shelter. The Act stipulates that the magistrate shall look on the application with 60 days from the first day of hearing. It provides for rights of women to secure and reside in her matrimonial house or shared household whether she has a title by the order of the magistrate.

A police officer, Protection Officer, service provider or Magistrate who has received a complaint of domestic violence or is otherwise present at the place of an incident of domestic violence or when the incident of domestic violence is reported to him, shall inform the aggrieved person-

(a) of her right to make an application for obtaining a relief by way of a protection order, an order for monetary relief, a custody order, a residence order, a compensation order or more than one such order under this Act;

(b) of the availability of services of service providers;

(c) of the availability of services of the Protection Officers;

(d) of her right to free legal services under the Legal Services Authorities Act, 1987 (39 of 1987);

(e) of her right to file a complaint under section 498A of the Indian Penal Code (45 of 1860), wherever relevant:

Provided that nothing in this Act shall be construed in any manner as to relieve a police officer from his duty to proceed in accordance with law upon receipt of information as to the commission of a cognizable offence.[xli]

The duty on part of person in charge of a shelter home and medical facility to provide its services upon the request by the aggrieved person or on her behalf a Protection Officer or Service Provider.[xlii]

A woman cannot be stopped from making a complaint/application alleging domestic violence. She has the right to the services and assistance of the Protection Officer and Service Providers, arranged under the provisions of the law. A woman who is the victim of domestic violence will have the right to the services of the police, shelter homes and medical establishments. She also has the right to simultaneously file her own complaint under Section 498A of the Indian Penal Code.[xliii]

One of the most important features of the Act is the woman's right to secure housing. The Act provides for the woman's right to reside in the matrimonial or shared household, whether or not she has any title or rights in the household. This right is secured by a residence order, which is passed by a court. These residence orders cannot be passed against anyone who is a woman. Even if she is a victim of domestic violence, she retains right to live in 'shared homes' that is, a home or homes she shares with the abusive partner. The law provides that if an abused woman requires, she has to be provided alternate accommodation and in such situations, the accommodation and her maintenance has to be paid for by her husband or partner. The law, significantly, recognizes the need of the abused woman for emergency relief, which will have to be provided by the husband.[xliv]

An important addition is that, law ensures that an aggrieved wife, who takes recourse to the law, cannot be harassed for doing so. Thus, if a husband is accused of any of the above forms of violence, he cannot during the pending disposal of the case prohibit/restrict the wife's continued access to resources/ facilities to which she is entitled by virtue of the domestic relationship, including access to the shared household. In short, a husband cannot take away her jewellery or money, or throw her out of the house while they are having a dispute.[xlv]

The Act establishes adequate machinery to ensure effective protection. The Act creates an extraordinary post of a Protection officer who is charged with the responsibility of taking expeditious steps for providing timely relief and it also grants authority to the Magistrate to give sufficient relief in the form of maintenance orders, custody orders and compensation. The Act also creates a novel agency called the 'service providers' who are entrusted with the job of filing Domestic Incident Reports with the Magistrate. The Act by itself does not punish the perpetrator of domestic violence. But if a case discloses any offences punishable under IPC, CRPC or Dowry prohibition Act, the Magistrate may then, frame appropriate charges to either try the case himself or he may commit it to Sessions Court if he may deem fit.[xlvi]

Under Section 31 of the Domestic Violence Act, a breach of protection order or of an interim protection order, by the perpetrator-respondent is an offence under the Act and is punishable with either simple or rigorous imprisonment for a term which may extend to one year or with fine which may extend to twenty thousand rupees or with both. The offence is cognizable and non-bailable. Upon the sole testimony of the woman, the Court may conclude that such an offence has been committed by the accused according to Section 32.

The Domestic Violence Act provides monetary compensation Protection Orders and Residence Orders. A Protection Order is a relief measure that is used in most domestic violence legislation internationally. It is a method by which domestic violence is sought to be curbed by issuing directions to the offender. Once domestic violence has been proved, a Residence Order details the living arrangements for the offender and the aggrieved in order to make sure that further violence is not perpetrated against the aggrieved.

Contribution of Judiciary

Making special provisions for women in respect of employment or posts under the State is an integral part of Article 15(3). This power conferred under Article 15(3), is not whittled down in any manner by Article 16.

In *Francis Coralie Mullin v. Union Territory Delhi, Administrator*[xlvii] the Supreme Court stated, any act which damages or injures or interferes with the use of any limb or faculty of a person, either permanently or even temporarily, would be within the inhibition of Article 21.

This meaning of the term life applies over the tortures subjected to the victims of domestic violence.

In *Ahmedabad Municipal Corporation v. Nawab Khan Gulab Khan*[xlviii], the Supreme Court emphasized the fact that the right to life included in its ambit the right to live with human dignity, basing its opinion on a host of cases that had been decided in favour of this proposition. The right to dignity would include the right against being subjected to humiliating sexual acts. It would also include the right against being insulted. These two facets of the right to life find mention under the definitions of sexual abuse and emotional abuse, respectively. A praiseworthy aspect of the legislation is the very conception of emotional abuse as a form of domestic violence. The recognition of sexual abuse of the wife by the husband as a form of violation to the person is creditable; especially as such sexual abuse is not recognized by the IPC as an offence. These acts would fall within the confines of domestic violence as envisaged by the Act, though the definition would not be limited to it.

In the cases of domestic violence sometimes the women is asked to leave her home. In *Chameli Singh v. State of U.P.*[xlix], it was held that the right to life would include the right to shelter. Under section 6, it is a duty of the Protection Officer to provide the aggrieved party accommodation where the party has no place of accommodation, on request by such party or otherwise. Under section 17, the party's right to continue staying in the shared household is protected. These provisions thereby enable women to use the various protections given to them without any fear of being left homeless.

In *Amalendu Bikash Saha & Ors vs Smt. Kalyani Saha & Ors*[l] section 2 of the Act defines domestic violence as "any act of physical, mental or sexual violence actually perpetrated or an attempt of such violence as well as the forcible restriction of individual freedom and of privacy, carried out against individuals who have or have had family or kinship ties or cohabit or dwell in the same home". This elaboration is important because it covers the aspect of privacy also which is often thought to be sofesticated and illusory.

The Delhi High Court in the case of *Varsha Kapoor v. Union of India and Others*,[li] Justice Sikri while considering the constitutionality of Domestic Violence Act held that-

"Keeping in mind that the DV Act has been held to be a valid piece of legislation giving power to the Parliament having regard to the provisions of Article 15 (3) of the Constitution which gives power to the Parliament to make such a law and thus, it is not ultra vires the legislative power of the Parliament. In order to provide such remedies, DV Act has been enacted. It is in this backdrop, we have to appreciate that married women (i.e. wives) are given rights to agitate their grievances against wide spectrum of respondents under proviso to Section 2(q) of the DV Act, with attempt to put an end to domestic violence and at the same time saving matrimonial home, which was not possible under the remedies provided in criminal law and there was no such provision under the existing Family Laws. When this was the lacuna in law sought to be plugged by passing the DV Act and the purpose was to remove the said mischief, leaving family relatives of a husband or a male partner out of purview of the "respondent" would negate the purpose for which the DV Act is passed.[lii] We, therefore, are of the opinion that a wife or a female living in a relationship in the nature of marriage belongs to "a well defined class". The legislation passes the test of permissible classification as both the conditions stand satisfied, viz., (i) classification is founded on intelligible differentia; and (ii) differential as a rational relation to the objective sought to be achieved by the statutes, i.e., DV Act."[liii]

In *Dennison Paulraj & Others vs. Union of India*,[liv] *the Court was of the opinion that* "Domestic violence is a worldwide phenomenon and has been discussed in International fora, including the Vienna Accord of 1994 and the Beijing Declaration and the Platform for Action (1995). The United Nations Committee Convention on Elimination of All Forms of Discrimination against Women (CEDAW) has recommended that States should act to protect women against violence of any kind, especially that occurring within the family. There is a perception, not unfounded or unjustified, that the lot and fate of women in India is an abjectly dismal one, which requires bringing into place, on an urgent basis, protective and ameliorative measures against exploitation of women. The argument that the Act is ultra vires the Constitution of India because it accords protection only to women and not to men is therefore, wholly devoid of any merit. We do not rule out the possibility of a man becoming the victim of domestic violence, but such cases would be few and far between, thus not requiring or justifying the protection of parliament."

In the case of *Sandhya Manoj Wankhde v. Manoj Bhimrao Wankhde and Ors*.[lv] Justice Altamas Kabir's observation in deciding whether a woman can be a respondent under Domestic Violence Act 2005. He allowed the appeal to set aside the impugned order of Bombay High Court Nagpur Bench saying under section 2(q) respondent to mean any adult male person, who is or has been in a domestic relationship with the aggrieved person, further the proviso widen the scope of definition including a relative of the husband or the male partner nowhere any restrictive meaning has been given to the expression of "relative" nor it says it is male specific. Therefore a woman can be a respondent being relative of adult male member.

In the case of *Smt Prabha Toppo v. State of Jharkhand*,[lvi] the court held that, Section 19 of the Act only protects the woman living in the house from being dispossessed from the said house and it also makes provision for alternate accommodation for the aggrieved person in appropriate cases. It no where prescribes that if the woman who is not residing in the house, or who is residing in a different house, her possession shall also be restored by the Court in exercise of the power under Section 19 of the said Act.

The Honourable Supreme Court in the case of *Vajresh Venkatray Anvekar* v. *State Of Karnataka* held that, it is one thing to say that every wear and tear of married life need not lead to suicide and it is another thing to put it so crudely and suggest that one or two assaults on a woman is an accepted social norm. Judges have to be sensitive to women's problems. Assault on a woman offends her dignity. What effect it will have on a woman depends on facts and circumstances of each case. There cannot be any generalization on this issue. Our observation, however, must not be understood to mean that in all cases of assault suicide must follow. Our objection is to the tenor of learned Sessions Judge's observations. We do not suggest that where there is no evidence the court should go out of its way, ferret out evidence and convict the accused in such cases. It is of course the duty of the court to see that an innocent person is not convicted. But it is equally the duty of the court to see that perpetrators of heinous crimes are brought to book. The above quoted extracts add to the reasons why learned Sessions Judge's judgment can be characterized as perverse. They show a mindset which needs to change. There is a phenomenal rise in crime against women and protection granted to women by the Constitution of India and other laws can be meaningful only if those who are entrusted with the job of doing justice are sensitized towards women's problems.[lvii]

In the case of *Savita Bhanot* v. *Lt. Col. V.D. Bhanot*[lviii] dealt with a case filed under the Domestic Violence Act and the Court came to the conclusion that the petition under the Domestic Violence was maintainable even if the Act of Domestic Violence have been committed prior to the coming into force of the Act

In the case of *Kavita Chaudhri* v. *Eveneet Singh And Anr* the court held that, with the transient course it has been observed that with the advent of various women friendly laws, empowering the women with equal rights as that of a man/ husband, the remedy of women to ask for maintenance or to claim her right in the residence in a commensurate property is only restricted to her husband and not against her parents in law. A woman is only[lix] entitled to claim a right to residence in a shared household, and a shared household would only mean the house belonging to or taken on rent by the husband, or the house which belongs to the joint family of which the husband is a member. This means that she can assert her rights, if any, only against the property of her husband and cannot claim a right to live in the house of her husband's parents without their wishes and caprice. Law permits a married woman to claim maintenance against her in- laws only in a situation covered under section 19 of The Hindu Adoption and Maintenance Act, 1956. i.e. after the death of the husband and that too when she is unable to maintain herself out of her own earnings etc. It would not be abominable to say that even the parents/ parents in law at the fag-end of their lives, deserve to live a blissful, happy and a peaceful life, away from any tautness or worries.

Conclusion

Judicial records show that the conviction rates in cases of domestic violence are very low and these records don't take into consideration those cases which never even make it to court.

Most of the cases of domestic violence remain hidden behind the four wall of the family because of family reputation, many poor innocent women even does not now or realize that they are victims of domestic violence and they think that this is the way of life. Many women bear all the kind of tortures because of the fake family reputations. Many do not object because they are financially dependent on their husbands and does not have any place to go. Most of the women also do not retaliate because they don't want to break the family for the sake of their children.

This is a fact that laws are not sufficient to deal with the problems like this. It is necessary to awaken the society and most specially the women. Making women aware of their rights is required. It is necessary to run legal awareness programmes in the remote areas. Along with that it is necessary to convince the family members to give just and humane treatment to the ladies in the family. There is a need to develop the culture to treat women at par with men. Along with the social reforms, all limbs of the government must also work sincerely to curb domestic violence. Especially the police must act promptly at such complaints and the judiciary also has a responsibility to resolve the cases speedily.

Essay-III

SEXUAL AND REPRODUCTIVE RIGHTS OF INDIAN WOMEN

Introduction

Reproductive rights are legal rights and freedoms relating to reproduction and reproductive health. The World Health Organization defines reproductive rights as follows:

Reproductive rights rest on the recognition of the basic right of all couples and individuals to decide freely and responsibly the number, spacing and timing of their children and to have the information and means to do so, and the right to attain the highest standard of sexual and reproductive health. They also include the right of all to make decisions concerning reproduction free of discrimination, coercion and violence.

Different kinds of rights constitute the sexual and reproductive rights which includes right to motherhood, protection from female infanticide, the right to legal or safe abortion, the right to birth control, right to access quality reproductive healthcare, and the right to education and access in order to make free and informed reproductive choices. Reproductive rights may also include the right to receive education about contraception and sexually transmitted infections, and freedom from coerced sterilization, abortion, and contraception, and protection from gender-based practices such as female genital mutilation (FGM) and male genital mutilation (MGM).The issues related to surrogate motherhood, live in relationship and single motherhood also belong to the territory of sexual and reproductive rights.

In a country like India where the society is closed it is a taboo in India to talk about sex. Female sexuality is still a more controversial sphere in the India society. Because of this situation women in India suffer from various social, psychological and health related problems. Sometimes the effects of this ignorance and non-accessibility are so grave that it results in shattering of their whole life, loss of health and relationship and sometimes life also.

Development of the concept -Reproductive rights began to develop as a subset of human rights at the United Nation's 1968 International Conference on Human Rights. [lx] The resulting non binding Proclamation of Teheran was the first international document to recognize one of these rights when it stated that: "Parents have a basic human right to determine freely and responsibly the number and the spacing of their children." [lxi]States, though, have been slow in incorporating these rights in internationally legally binding instruments. Thus, while some of these rights have already been recognized in hard law, that is, in legally binding international human rights instruments, others have been mentioned only in non binding recommendations and, therefore, have at best the status of soft law in international law, while a further group is yet to be accepted by the international community and therefore remains at the level of advocacy. [lxii]

In 1945, the UN Charter included the obligation "to promote... universal respect for, and observance of, human rights and fundamental freedoms for all without discrimination as to race, sex, language, or religion". However, the Charter did not define these rights. Three years later, the UN adopted the Universal Declaration of Human Rights (UDHR), the first international legal document to delineate human rights; the UDHR does not mention reproductive rights. Reproductive rights began to appear as a subset of human rights in the 1968 Proclamation of Teheran.

This right was affirmed by the UN General Assembly in the 1974 Declaration on Social Progress and Development. According to this declaration the family as a basic unit of society and the natural environment for the growth and well-being of all its members, particularly children and youth, should be assisted and protected so that it may fully assume its responsibilities within the community. Parents have the exclusive right to determine freely and responsibly the number and spacing of their children. The 1975 UN International Women's Year Conference echoed the Proclamation of Teheran.

Later the twenty year "Cairo Programme of Action" was adopted in 1994 at the International Conference on Population and Development (ICPD) in Cairo. The non binding Programme of Action asserted that governments have a responsibility to meet individuals' reproductive needs, rather than demographic targets. It recommended that Family planning services be provided in the context of other reproductive health services, including services for healthy and safe childbirth, care for sexually transmitted infections, and post-abortion care. The ICPD also addressed issues such as violence against women, sex trafficking, and adolescent health.[lxiii] The Cairo Program is the first international policy document to define reproductive health, stating:

Reproductive health is a state of complete physical, mental and social well-being and not merely the absence of disease or infirmity, in all matters relating to the reproductive system and its functions and processes. Reproductive health therefore implies that people are able to have a satisfying and safe sex life and that they have the capability to reproduce and the freedom to decide if, when and how often to do so. Implicit in this last condition are the right of men and women to be informed [about] and to have access to safe, effective, affordable and acceptable methods of family planning of their choice, as well as other methods for regulation of fertility which are not against the law, and the right of access to appropriate health-care services that will enable women to go safely through pregnancy and childbirth and provide couples with the best chance of having a healthy infant.

In 1999, recommendations at the ICPD were expanded to include commitment to AIDS education, research, and prevention of mother-to-child transmission, as well as to the development of vaccines and microbicides. [lxiv]

The 1995 Fourth World Conference on Women in Beijing, in its non-binding Declaration and Platform for Action, supported the Cairo Programme's definition of reproductive health, but established a broader context of reproductive rights to include their right to have control over and decide freely and responsibly on matters related to their sexuality, including sexual and reproductive health, free of coercion, discrimination and violence. Equal relationships between women and men in matters of sexual relations and reproduction, including full respect for the integrity of the person, require mutual respect, consent and shared responsibility for sexual behavior and its consequences.

The Beijing Platform demarcated twelve interrelated critical areas of the human rights of women that require advocacy. The Platform framed women's reproductive rights as "indivisible, universal and inalienable human rights."

The Yogyakarta Principles

The Yogyakarta Principles on the Application of International Human Rights Law in relation to Sexual Orientation and Gender Identity, proposed by a group of experts in November 2006[14] but not yet incorporated by States in international law,[15] declares in its Preamble that "the international community has recognized the rights of persons to decide freely and responsibly on matters related to their sexuality, including sexual and reproductive health, free from coercion, discrimination, and violence." In relation to reproductive health, Principle 9 on "The Right to Treatment with Humanity while in Detention" requires that "States shall... [p]rovide adequate access to medical care and counseling appropriate to the needs of those in custody, recognizing any particular needs of persons on the basis of their sexual orientation and gender identity, including with regard to reproductive health, access to HIV/AIDS information and therapy and access to hormonal or other therapy as well as to gender-reassignment treatments where desired."[16] Nonetheless, African, Caribbean and Islamic Countries, as well as the Russian Federation, have objected to the use of these principles as Human Rights standards.

Indian Scene

India is a closed society. Taking about sex or sexual and reproductive matters is a taboo here .The Constitution of India guarantees equality of sexes and in fact grants special favours to women. These can be found in three articles of the Constitution. Article 14 says that the government shall not deny to any person equality before law or the equal protection of the laws. Article 15 declares that government shall not discriminate against any citizen on the ground of sex. Article 15 (3) makes a special provision, enabling the State to make affirmative discriminations in favour of women. Moreover, the government can pass special laws in favour of women... Article 21, right to life and personal liberty is interpreted by the court to cover the dignity of women also. Above all, the Constitution imposes a fundamental duty on every citizen through Articles 51 (A) (e) to renounce the practices derogatory to the dignity of women.[lxv] All these provisions equip the Indian constitution with the requirements to safeguard the sexual and reproductive rights. The principle of gender equality which are enshrined in the Indian Constitution in its Preamble, Fundamental Rights, Fundamental Duties and Directive Principles of State Policy. The Constitution not only guarantees equality to women, but also empowers the State to adopt measures of positive discrimination in favour of women. Since the Fifth Five Year Plan (1974-78), India has been making a marked shift in its approach to women's issues from welfare to development while keeping the empowerment of women as the central issue in determining their status in the society. The National Commission for Women was set up by an Act of Parliament in 1990 to safeguard the rights and legal entitlements of women. The 73rd and 74th Amendments to the Constitution in 1993 have provided for reservation of seats in the local bodies of Panchayats and Municipalities for women, laying a strong foundation for their participation in decision-making at the local levels. India has also ratified various international conventions and human rights instruments committing to secure equal rights of women. Key among them is the ratification of the Convention on Elimination of All Forms of Discrimination Against Women (CEDAW) in 1993. [lxvi]

In the Indian society the sexual and reproductive rights are on a lower footing. The prevention of Child marriage Act, settles the 18 years as the minimum age of marriage for girls. The purpose is to delay the burden of sexual and child bearing responsibilities; however the custom of child marriage is still prevailing secretly. 'Akshaya tritiya' is the day on which community child marriages are observed in may communities. Few years back both the hands of lady social worker working with the women and child development department were cut because she tried to stop child marriages in a town. The young girls are thrown open to sexual abuse by their husband in the name of marriage. They have no knowledge of sex or childbirth. They are neither emotionally nor physically mature for this life. This results in diseases, trauma, abortions and even death.

On the other hand cast based arranged marriages are observed as a rule in the society. If some girls desire to have a relationship or to marry a boy outside the community it is not acceptable by the society. The anger of the society is reflected in many forms including 'honor killings'.[lxvii]

The United Nations Population Fund (UNFPA) and the World Health Organization (WHO) advocate for reproductive rights with a primary emphasis on women's rights. In this respect the UN and WHO focus on a range of issues from access to family planning services, sex education, menopause, and the reduction of obstetric fistula, to the relationship between reproductive health and economic status.

The reproductive rights of women are advanced in the context of the right to freedom from discrimination and the social and economic status of women. Control over reproduction is a basic need and a basic right for all women. Linked as it is to women's health and social status, as well as the powerful social structures of religion, state control and administrative inertia, and private profit, it is from the perspective of poor women that this right can best be understood and affirmed. Women know that childbearing is a social, not a purely personal, phenomenon; nor do we deny that world population trends are likely to exert considerable pressure on resources and institutions by the end of this century.

In order to empower women Article 39 talks about the certain principles of policy that need to be followed by the state which are securing adequate means of livelihood equally for men and women, equal pay for equal work among men and women, and the health and strength of workers, men and women are not abused. Article 42 requires the state to make provision for securing humane conditions of work and maternity relief.

Attempts have been made to analyze the socioeconomic conditions that affect the realization of a woman's reproductive rights. The term reproductive justice has been used to describe these broader social and economic issues. Proponents of reproductive justice argue that while the right to legalized abortion and contraception applies to everyone, these choices are only meaningful to those with resources, and that there is a growing gap between access and affordability.

In *C.B. Muthamma v. Union of India* [lxviii] the validity of the Indian Foreign Service (Conduct an discipline) Rules of 1961 was challenged which provided that a female employee to obtain a written permission of the Government in writing before her marriage is solemnized and at any time after a marriage a women member of the service may be required to resign from service. The Supreme Court held that such provision is discriminatory against women and hence unconstitutional.

In *Vishakha and others v. State of Rajasthan* [lxix], the Supreme Court held that sexual harassment of working women at her place of an employment amounts to violation of rights of gender equality and right to life and liberty which is clear violation of Article 14, 15 and 21 of the Indian Constitution. The Court further observed that the meaning and content of the fundamental rights guaranteed in the Constitution of India are of sufficient amplitude to encompass all the facts of gender equality including prevention of sexual harassment or abuse.
Economic dependence of women is what gives rise to their subordination in society today. Hence to remove such subordination and lay the foundation of equality women too must be made economically independent and must take an active role in all sectors of business today. Problem faced by women in the economic sphere of life are mostly relating to unequal wages and discrimination resulting from their biological role in nature of childbearing. To curb such problems and protect the economic rights of women the legislature introduced the Equal Remuneration Act, 1976 and Maternity Benefit Act, 1961.

A maternity benefit is one that every woman shall be entitled to, and her employer shall be liable for, the payment of maternity benefit, which is the amount payable to her at the rate of average daily wages for the period of her actual absence. The Maternity Benefit Act aims to regulate of employment of women in certain establishment for certain periods before and after childbirth and provides for maternity and certain benefits.

Women can claim benefits under the act everywhere except in factories and the other establishment where the Employee's State Insurance Act is applicable. Women who are employed, whether directly or through a contractor, have actually worked in the establishment for a period of at least 80 days during the 12 months are eligible to claim the benefits under this act. Cash benefits to women who are absent from work during the maternity leave, are not be less than two-thirds of her previous earnings.

Discharge or dismissal during maternity leave is considered to be void. When pregnant women absents herself from work in accordance with the provision of this act, it shall be unlawful for her employer to discharge or dismiss her during, or on account of, such absence, or give notice of discharge or dismissal in such a day that notice will expire during such absence or vary to her disadvantage any of the conditions of her services. Dismissal or discharge of a pregnant woman shall not disentitle her to the maternity benefit or medical bonus allowable under the act except if it was on some other ground.

Failure to pay maternity benefits or discharge or unemployment of woman due to maternity will result in imprisonment of the employer for not less than three months which may extend to one year and a fine of rupees two hundred which may extend to five thousand.

In the *B. Shah v. P.O.*[lxx] case it was held that 100% wages were to be provided for all days of leave as well as benefits such as Sundays and rest days as wages were being for actual number of working days missed.

In *Air India v. Nargesh Mirza* [lxxi], the Supreme Court struck down the provision of rules which stipulated termination of service of an air hostess on her first pregnancy as it arbitrary and abhorrent to the notions of a civilized society. the first Air Hostess case, apart from other questions, the legality of regulation 46(c) was challenged. This regulation provided superannuation of an Air Hostess at the age of 35 years or on marriage if it takes place within four years of service or on first pregnancy, whichever is earlier. The court declared the provision for retirement on first pregnancy to be unreasonable and said, 'Whether the woman after bearing children would continue in service or would find it difficult to look after the children is her personal matter and a problem which affects the Air Hostess concerned and the

Corporation has nothing to do with the same.'

The ongoing argument in some circles is that the wage differential between women and men is caused by the need to compensate the higher labour costs employers incur by hiring women, in accordance with special laws to protect maternity. Employers prefer to hire a male instead of female, without the burden of these additional monetary costs. This is however not enough as many employers do not hire married women or dismiss them before pregnancy. The act provides some protection to women economically especially today in an age where single mothers are becoming more prevalent it gives them stability in their lives to have their wages and the security of returning to a steady job. My personal views are that this act is not enough to guarantee women equality and economic security but it is definitely a starting step and though there are several bridges to cross.

Even for women employed in the organized sector, child care service is very conspicuous by its absence. Very scanty service is available in some urban areas. The reproductive role of women and the frequency of child bearing push them out of the labour market in a substantial part of their productive period. This hampers their economic contribution very significantly. The increasing awareness of family planning will be a measure of empowerment for women, releasing them for activities of their choice for a longer period of their lives.

In *Mrs. Neera Mathur vs. Life Insurance Corporation of India*[lxxii]. Neera Mathur was a probationer in the Life Insurance Corporation (LIC). During probation she applied and was granted maternity leave. She was simply discharged from service after she returned. Her discharge was defended by the LIC on the ground that she had given false declaration at the stage of entering the service. The court held that 'the particulars to be furnished under columns (iii) to (viii) in the declaration are indeed embarrassing if not humiliating.' These columns were held unreasonable and discharge was set aside.

In *Punjab National Bank by Chairman and another v. Astamija Dash* [lxxiii], it was held that as per provision of the maternity benefit Act, 1961 a woman can avail leave during the period of six weeks from the day immediately following the day of her delivery, miscarriage or medical termination of pregnancy. If request is made by herself she would not be asked to work for the period specified as per section 4(4). She would be entitled to the benefits of section 6 and 9 of the Act.

Stringent laws are present in India to prevent unsafe and unnecessary abortions. Under the Indian Penal Code 1860 causing miscarriage is a crime. Whoever voluntarily causes a woman with child to miscarry, shall if such miscarriage be not caused in good faith for the purpose of saving the life of the woman, be punished with imprisonment of either description for a term which may extend to three years, or with fine, or with both; and, if the woman be quick with child, shall be punished with imprisonment of either description for a term which may extend to seven years, and shall also be liable to fine. A woman who causes herself to miscarry, is within the meaning of this section.

Death caused by act done with intent to cause miscarriage, of a woman with child, does any act which causes the death of such woman, shall be punished with imprisonment of either description for a term which may extend to ten years, and shall also be liable to fine; if act done without woman's consent, if act done without woman's consent and if the act is done without the consent of the woman, shall be punished either with imprisonment for life. It is not essential to this offence that the offender should know that the act is likely to cause death. Act done with intent to prevent child being born alive or to cause it to die after birth or whoever before the birth of any child does any act with the intention of thereby preventing that child from being born alive or causing it to die after its birth, and does by such

Causing death of quick unborn child by act is amounting to culpable homicide. Whoever does any act under such circumstances, that if he thereby caused death he would be guilty of culpable homicide, and does by such act cause the death of a quick unborn child, shall be punished with imprisonment of either description for a term which may extend to ten years, and shall also be liable to fine.

Under the Medical Termination of Pregnancy Act also the law relating to abortions is very clear,it was 1971 was passed on 10th August1971. This Act is to provide for the termination of certain pregnancies by registered medical practitioners and for matters connected there with or incidental thereto. According to this Act a registered medical practitioner shall not be guilty of any offence under that code or under nay other law for the time being in force, if any pregnancy is terminated by him in accordance with the provisions of this Act. The Act mentions that where the length of the pregnancy does not exceed twelve weeks, it can be terminated at the advice if one registered medical practitioner, if such medical practitioner, is, or where the length of the pregnancy exceeds twelve weeks but does not exceed twenty weeks, if not less than two registered medical practitioners are, of opinion formed in good faith, that (i) the continuance of the pregnancy would involve a risk to the life of the pregnant woman or of grave injury to her physical or mental health; or (ii) there is a substantial risk that if the child were born it would be suffer form such physical or mental abnormalities as to be seriously handicapped. The Act also explains that No termination of pregnancy shall be made in accordance with this act at any place other than (a) a hospital established or maintained by Government, or (b) a place for the time being approved for the purpose of this Act by Government.

Another important legislation is the Pre Natal Diagnostic Techniques(Regulation and Prevention of Misuse) Act, 1994 which was passed on the 20th September, 1994. This is an act to provide for the regulation of the use of pre-natal diagnostic techniques for the purpose of detecting genetic or metabolic disorders or chromosomal abnormalities or certain congenital malformations or sex linked disorders and for the prevention of the misuse of such techniques for the purpose of pre-natal sex determination leading to female foeticide; and for matters connected therewith or incidental thereto. According to the provisions of this Act no Genetic Counselling Centre or Genetic Laboratory or Genetic clinic shall conduct or cause to be conducted in its Centre Laboratory or Clinic pre-natal diagnostic techniques including ultrasonography for the purpose of determining the sex of the foetus and no person shall conduct or cause to be conducted any pre-natal; diagnostic techniques including ultrasonography for the purpose of determining the sex of foetus.

I the light of this discussion it is relevant to mention the comment of Lara Knudsen who is a pro-choice activist, she has suggested that "twenty percent of all pregnancies worldwide end in abortion, and nearly half of those abortions are unsafe and often illegal." According to the WHO, more than 45 million (legal and illegal) abortions take place annually. At the same time, approximately 66,500 women die from the complications of unsafe abortion every year. In India the problem is even grave. Because of the socio-religious reasons son preference is common in the society this is one of the grave reason of the violation of sexual and reproductive rights of the women. Every family awaits birth of a boy. The sex of the baby is determined by pre natal diagnostic techniques and the child is illegally aborted if it happens to be a girl. Mother has no say in the decision. She is taken just as machinery to reproduce. These illegal abortions sometimes also result in injury or death of the women.

Family planning, number and spacing of children are usually not a decision by the women; all these issues are decided by the husband or the male folk in the families. In some families due to religious reasons family planning is not advised and the women are compelled to give births to dozens of children as long as they are having reproductive capacity.

The women are not allowed to use or select the contraceptives or to take the medical advice of gynecologist in these matters. Women catch the sexually transmitted diseases from their partners; they don't have any awareness or knowledge about the health and hygiene and due to a taboo in accessing the gynecologists women often develop various infections which aggravate in the form of deadly diseases.

The World Health Organization calls for safe, legal abortion a "fundamental right of women, irrespective of where they live" and unsafe abortion a "silent pandemic". Access to safe abortion improves women's health. In India where abortion has been legal for decades, access to competent care remains restricted because of other barriers. The WHO's Development and Research Training in Human Reproduction (HRP), whose research concerns people's sexual and reproductive health and lives, has an overall strategy to combat unsafe abortion that comprises four inter-related activities:

to collate, synthesize and generate scientifically sound evidence on unsafe abortion prevalence and practices; to develop improved technologies and implement interventions to make abortion safer; to translate evidence into norms, tools and guidelines; and to assist in the development of programmes and policies that reduce unsafe abortion and improve access to safe abortion and high quality post abortion care. Department of health and family welfare has adopted the national health Policy 2012. The mission of the department includes the target to stabilize the population of India by the year 2025, to ensure gender balance I every section of the society, to reduce infant mortality rate to 28 per 1000 live births and to reduce the maternal mortality ratio to 1 per 1000 live births.

Schemes of Ministry of Women & Child Development, Govt. of India. "Ujjawala" is a comprehensive scheme for prevention of Trafficking and Rescue, Rehabilitation and Re-integration of Victims of Trafficking for commercial Sexual Exploitation.

"Ladli lakshmi" and "kishori shakti "schemes are major scheme for girls. A national programme for adolescent girls is run and financial assistance to lactating mothers of poor sections is also undertaken.

Government of Madhya Pradesh is also running various schemes for protecting women, 'Mukhya mantri kayadan yojana' is used to ensure that child marriage is not done ad community marriages without dowry are performed.

'Anganbris' are established at every locality in villages and urban areas where the eduated young girls are employed (who are called' Asha didi') to educate women in relation of their sexual and reproductive health. The programmes run there includes distribution of sanitary napkins at a nominal rate, distribution of essential medicines, pre marriage counseling including teaching the family planning measures and giving psychological support, distribution of iron and potassium tablets to pregnant women, awareness about proper diet, iodine deficiency etc., educating people about gender equality so that female feticide may be stopped, running of 'goud-bharai' scheme (under which a function is arranged to celebrate and register the pregnancy), motivating the deliveries to be done in hospitals or health care centers, giving of special allowance to motivate hospital deliveries, running of free vehicles to pick and drop women from hospital before and after delivery, (these vehicals afe called 'Janani- express'), distribution of daliya to lactating mothers, educating women to maintain spacing between the children, motivating couples to get sterilization done after two children, awareness of breast cancer, free breast cancer check up camps, AIDS awareness programmes and medication, mainstreaming sex workers, providing medical, financial and psychological support to victims of sexual offences etc.

These all schemes of the government and support and participation of civil society and non- governmental organizations have generated a hope for better future of Indian womanhood. New way of thoughts like legalization of live in relationships to safeguard the status of women who have dedicated there lives to their male partners and are in sexual relationships with them are new but debated issues in the Indian strata. The live in women did not get any protection from exploitation and could not claim ay right against their male partner only because of the fact that their social status is falling less than that of the legally wedded wife. Court has given justice to such women by imposing the obligation on the male partner to maintain such women so that he could not escape his responsibility and take advantage of the fact that the women he lived with was not his wife.

Sexual and reproductive rights are very fundamental and essential ingredients of the right to life. Recognition of these rights in the society has opened the gates of their protection and growth also. Social support is the first and legal remedies are the second tool to preserve, protect and prevent the violation of sexual and reproductive rights of Indian women.

ESSAY-IV

INTERNALLY DISPLACED PERSONS AND HUMAN RIGHTS

Introduction

Since the beginning of civilization individuals are forced from their homes as a result of armed conflict, generalized violence, human rights violations or natural or human-made disasters. In the modern world such persons who have not crossed an internationally recognized State border but are displaced within their own country are called Internally Displaced Persons. Internally Displaced Persons are among very vulnerable group of people because they don't have money or assets, they also don't know the language and culture of the sites where they enter. Unlike refugees, Internally Displaced Persons have not crossed an international border to find sanctuary but have remained inside their home countries. Although they remain entitled to the same rights as other citizens within their own country, in reality, the displacement can increase their vulnerability to human rights violations which include rape, exploitations and forced recruitment and also their needs including shelter, replacement of documentation and restitution of property. Internally Displaced Persons may also face administrative, institutional and procedural obstacles in achieving their rights. They have lost their documentation, for example, ration cards, domicile certificates, educational degrees, bank records etc, they have also left their real and movable properties in their native places. Due to this they not be able to take part in elections; not able to avail the benefit of governmental schemes, they may be deprived of education and other facilities also.

The United Nations first recognized the phenomenon of internal displacement in1988 when it convened the International Conference on the Plight of Refugees, Returnees and Displaced Persons in Southern Africa generally referred to as the Oslo Conference). In (the two decades since, international attention to the subject has grown considerably. The promulgation and official recognition of the Guiding Principles on Internal Displacement as well as efforts to improve the response to the protection and material needs of the Internally Displaced in the context of United Nations humanitarian reform initiatives attest to this growing concern. The Guiding Principles define Internally Displaced Persons as "persons or groups of persons who have been forced or obliged to flee or to leave their homes or places of habitual residence, in particular as a result of or in order to avoid the effects of armed conflict, situations of generalized violence, violation of human rights or natural or man-made disasters and who have not crossed an internationally recognized State border". This definition is noteworthy as it focuses on flight from armed conflict and human rights violations and includes flight from disasters rather than limiting itself to flight from a well-founded fear of persecution.

The gradual recognition of internal displacement as a global challenge derived from the sheer growth in the numbers of Internally Displaced than compared to refugees whose claim international protection is as enshrined in the 1951 Convention Relating to the Status of Refugees and its 1967 protocol. World War-II created massive internal displacement and hundreds of thousands of people in Europe and Asia remained in "displacement camps" in its immediate aftermath. As these people returned to their homes or sought new lives in foreign countries, internal displacement diminished as humanitarian challenge. The international system that emerged after World War-II predicted on the existence of sovereign states with clearly defined borders and thus emerging conflicts would be a inter-state rather that internal. In this context, the Refugee Convention reflected the assumption that persons seeking refugee from a well-founded fear of persecution would find it by crossing an international border into a foreign state. The drafters of the Refugee Convention did not anticipate the exponential rise in internal conflicts which became especially widespread in the 1980s and the inability of individuals Displaced by these conflicts to seek or to find asylum in neighboring countries.

Global Policy

The official attention to the issue of internal displacement emerged from the United Nations Human Rights Commission. It passed a resolution in1991 mandating a study of the issue. The following year the commission approved the resolution and asked the Secretary-General to appoint a representative to seek views and information from all governments on the human rights issue related to Internally Displaced Persons. The resolution mandated the representative to examine international human rights, humanitarian and refugee law and its applicability to the protection of and relief assistance to the Internally Displaced. The Secretary -General was asked to present such findings in a comprehensive report which would identify existing mechanisms relevant to Internally Displaced Persons protection as well as proposal for ways to fill up any gaps in the international protection regime. Among the member states of the Human Rights Committee a decision was taken to mandate a representative rather than a working group or rapporteur, along with a mere report. Furthermore, the position of the representative was unpaid and carried with it no special support staff. The chosen person would be expected to work on his or her own time while balancing other commitments. Secretary-General chose Sudanese diplomat, Francis Deng, as his representative on Internally Displaced Persons. For policy and logistical support, Francis Deng was able to convince his organizational home, the Washington-based Brookings Institution, to establish a special report on internal displacement headed by Roberta Cohen, a former U.S. State Department official and non-governmental analyst with experience in human rights and refugee issues. Francis Deng in close partnership with Roberta Cohen and other colleagues turned what could have been a dead assignment into a twelve years effort that dramatically increased the global recognition of and commitment to the protection and assistance needs of Internally Displaced people.

The fundamental problem was unlike refugees, Internally Displaced Persons did not benefit from specific legal protection embodied in an internationally recognized convention with official state parties. Furthermore, unlike the Office of the United Nations High Commission for Refugee (UNHCR), no single agency existed for the express purpose of protecting them and providing them with material assistance. Finally, Internally Displacement Persons protection, more so than that of refugee, involved directly the question of infringement on State sovereign. From the outset of Francis Deng's work a legal framework for Internally Displaced Persons was developed. The initial consultations with government officials, experts in international human rights and humanitarian law and representatives of organizations such as United Nations Human Rights Commission, the International Organization for Migration (IOM) and the International Committee of the Red Cross (ICRC) made it clear that concern existed about creating a new category of people requiring special international protection. In this context, developing the equivalent of a convention for Internally Displaced Persons was too ambitious. Given particularly state commitment to the idea of sovereignty, the only tenable approach was to consolidate existing norms in international human rights and humanitarian law relevant to the protection of Internally Displaced Persons, to identify and seek to fill any gaps, and to issue a document designed to both provide authoritative guidance and raise awareness. Francis Deng and a team of international legal experts worked for five years on the Guiding Principles on Internally Displacement, in which Francis Deng's introductory note was "identify the rights and guarantees relevant to the protection of the Internally Displaced in all phases of displacement". In 1988 they were endorsed by the Inter-Agency Standing Committee, which brings together the heads of the United Nation humanitarian organizations, the International Committee of the Red Cross (ICRC), International Organization for Migration (IOM) and non-governmental organizations (NGOs) represented by two major consortia, the International Council of Voluntary Agencies based in Geneva, Switzerland and Inter Action based in Washington, D.C. At the same time, the guidelines were noted in a resolution of the Human Rights Committee.

The Guiding Principles focus on flight from armed conflict and human rights violations and includes flight from disasters rather than limiting itself to flight from a well-founded fear of persecution. In doing so, the Guiding Principles incorporated expansions of the refugee definition that had become accepted in International Human Rights law and practice, drawing on the Organization of African Unity's Convention Governing the Specific Aspects of Refugee Problems in Africa (1969) and the Cartagena Declaration on Refugees (1984). These agreements by regional organizations accepted that individuals fleeing due to generalized violence, internal conflicts, foreign aggression or occupation and events disrupting the public order should qualify as refugees. The Guiding Principles are comprehensive. They assert in the first principle that Internally Displaced Persons shall enjoy "the same rights and freedoms under international and domestic law as do other persons in their country". Other general principles include recognition of the primary duty and responsibility of national authorities to provide protection and humanitarian assistance to the Internally Displaced within their jurisdiction and recognition of the special needs of children, expectant mothers, female heads of the households, people with disabilities and the elderly. Subsequent sections define principles and the rights of Internally Displaced Persons relating to protection from displacement; protection during displacement; humanitarian assistance and return, resettlement and reintegration. In some cases the Guiding Principles draw strong prohibitions and protections that already exist in human rights law. For example, the right to life includes nonderogable (meaning no exceptions are permitted) guarantees prohibiting genocide, arbitrary executions and indiscriminate and disproportionate attacks on civilians. Similarly, the right to personal integrity which is also non-derogable is infringed by torture, cruel and disregarding punishment and rape. These non-derogable rights are embodied in Principles 10 and 11, the first two principles in the section on protection during displacement. The point was to stress that certain rights could not be suspended even in armed conflict, a national emergency or other exceptional situations that might be declared by government.

The most significant international recognition of the Guiding Principles has been their inclusion in the General Assembly's resolution on the 2005 World Summit Outcome. The World Summit brought together heads of state on the occasion of the fiftieth anniversary of the United Nation. Paragraph 132 of the resolution states: "We recognize the Guiding Principles on Internal Displacement as an important international framework for the protection of Internally Displaced Persons and resolve to take effective measures to increase the protection of Internally Displaced Persons". This acknowledgement of the importance of Guiding Principles represents a significant advance, considering the reservations held by many countries on the merits of focusing on internal displacement when the effort first started in the early 1990s.[lxxiv]

Internally Displaced Persons in India

In india the main reasons for displacement are armed conflict, developmental projects, naxalism, militancy, linguistic discrimination, situations of generalized violence, violation of human rights or natural or man-made disasters. Internal displacement can affect persons in particular or an entire group which covers a wide range of possibilities of being expelled by force or intimidated to leave by threat or necessity. But the most important fact is that displacement is coerced or involuntary. Though there can be different issues which leads to internal displacement of persons, the causes can be brought under two broad heads. They are:

a) Displacement due to internal conflict and

b) Displacement due to development

a) Displacement Due to Internal Conflict:

Forced internal displacements are an acute and sensitive issue. Internally Displaced Persons often lost all their properties and are obliged to start a new life without perspective of safe return, resettlement, or compensation as they are forced to leave their original place of living. There are different parts of India where such situation has taken into place and some of the situations are as follows:

Persons displaced from Jammu and Kashmir- India's largest situation regarding Internally Displaced Persons stems out from the conflict in the north-western state of Jammu & Kashmir between militants seeking either independence or accession to Pakistan. The status of Kashmir has been challenged since the creation of independent India and Pakistan in 1947 and the two countries have twice gone to war over the issue. However, security has improved with the ceasefire concluded in November 2003; Islamic militant groups have continued to launch attacks against local authorities and civilians to sabotage the peace process. Since 1989, the insurgency in Indian administered Kashmir has claimed at least 67,000 lives.[lxxv] In Kashmir Valley, more than 90 percent of Hindu populations-the Kashmiri Pandits remain Internally Displaced as a result of this conflict. The government estimated that 250,000 fled from the Valley during the 1990s, while Pandit groups believe at least 350,000 people were displaced. Today, around 100,000 live in the capital New Delhi and some 240,000 in the city of Jammu.[lxxvi]. Protection of the remaining Pandit population has been far from adequate, leading to further displacement during 2004 when 160 of the estimated 700 Pandit families remaining in the Kashmir Valley fled an upsurge of violence and killings.[lxxvii]

Displacement in North East-Sister States- The eight states in the geographically isolated and economically underdeveloped North-East are home to 200 of the 430 tribal groups in India. 30 to 40 rebel groups are currently active in this region. During the past decades, the Northeast has been the scene of repeated ethnically- motivated conflicts in which the fight for a perceived homeland has sometimes resulted in ethnic cleansing. At least 50,000 people have been killed in such conflicts in the Northeast since India's independence in 1947.[lxxviii] Violence has broken out in the states of Assam, Manipur, Nagaland, Tripura and Arunachal Pradesh, involving at least ten different ethnic groups (Bodos, Nagas, Kukis, Karbis, Dimasas, Paites, Mizos, Reangs, Bengalis and Chakmas). The largest forced displacement movements have occurred in the states of Assam, Manipur and Tripura.[lxxix] During 2005, thousands of Muslims of Bengali origin were driven out by angry mobs, accused of being illegal migrants from Bangladesh.[lxxx] Major waves of displacement have also occurred due to violence against seasonal workers, mainly from Bengal. In November 2003, communal violence Displaced at least 18,000 people who fled to about 40 camps in and outside Assam.[lxxxi] At least 10,000 people have been killed in separatist violence in Assam over the past 25 years.[lxxxii] The largest displacement situation in the state stems from the fighting between Bodos and Santhals, which erupted in the early 1990s and Displaced an estimated 250,000 persons. As of December 2005, around 110,000 people remained in relief camps in Assam's Kokrajhar and Gossaigaon subdivisions – a decrease of 40,000 people since 2003. However, the Displaced have not been able to return to their former villages, as they remain occupied, mainly by Bodo communities. Tribal leaders say they were forced out of the relief camps because the state authorities decided to stop all humanitarian assistance. Today, they are landless and destitute.[lxxxiii] . The Karbi Anglong and North Cachar Hills districts of Assam have been the main scenes of ethnic violence in recent years. Thousands of civilians have been displaced mainly due to fighting between Karbi, Kuki and Dimasa insurgent groups. In October 2005, there were clashes between the rival Karbi and Dimasa tribes, which continued until the end of the year Up to 50,000 people from both tribes, were Displaced and took shelter mainly in public buildings situated in safer areas.[lxxxiv] In Manipur, counter-insurgency operations by the Indian army against local groups along the border with Burma (Myanmar), as well as ethnic clashes, have resulted in the displacement of at least 6,000 people from the Hmar and Paite ethnic groups. Like Internally Displaced Persons elsewhere in the Northeast, they are also reported to live in deplorable conditions, lacking food, medicines, warm clothes and other essential commodities.[lxxxv] In northern Tripura, it is estimated that insurgent groups internally displace more than 100,000 people due to ethnic fighting and attacks. The main pattern of displacement is attack on villages inhabited by people of Bengali origin. Considered foreigners by the local tribal population, they have increasingly become the target of local armed groups.[lxxxvi] Other populations at risk of displacement in the Northeast are the Chakmas who are regularly threatened with expulsion, in particular by an influential Arunachal student's organization, which maintains that the Chakmas should be resettled elsewhere.[lxxxvii] Although conflicts regularly displace people in the Northeast, no official estimate exists. Most information is found in local newspapers, while objective research in terms of assessing the magnitude of conflict-induced displacement in the region has yet to be carried out by either governmental or non-governmental agencies.[lxxxviii]

Displacement of Nepalis - The process of migration of the Nepalis in Northeast India, Darjeeling, and Southern Bhutan began about two centuries ago with the recruitment of Gorkha soldiers into the British Indian Army after the treaty of Sugauli (1816). The British who wanted a hardy labour force for their tea plantations facilitated the Nepali migration to Darjeeling while in Sikkim, the Nepalis served as a wedge to contain the Bhutias. Anti-Nepali feeling in Northeast India was first observed during the Assam Movement. While the targets were the illegal migrants from Bangladesh, the Nepalis were also included in the anti-foreigner discourse. Allegations of Nepalis from Northeast India crossing over to side with the Lhotshampas and of their leaders, fleeing to Assam, probably encouraged the targeting of Nepalis in Northeast India in ethnic assertions and backlashes. They were largely caught in the crossfire between the Assamese anti-foreigner agitation and the Bodo Movement. Although the government of India had clarified its position on the Nepalis early in February 1984 - that those in possession of the Restricted Area Permit would not come within the definition of 'illegal migrants' and stood protected - their position was soon threatened by the agitation for a separate Bodoland. In Manipur, the sentiment took the form of a movement that in 1980 manifested itself in direct attacks on the Nepalis, compelling many of them to relocate and flee to safer areas. Meghalaya saw similar sectarian violence in 1987. The violence primarily targeted the Nepali minority living in Shillong, Jowai and other parts of Meghalaya, which had over 150,000 Nepalis. Most of the Nepali people fled but the worst affected were the dairy farmers who had to give up their occupation and leave the state. Today, most of the Displaced from Meghalaya and Manipur are settled in Rupandehi, Jhapa, Banke and other parts of Nepal's Terai region, besides Kathmandu and Pokhara. The anti-foreigner upsurge also spread to Mizoram and Nagaland where again Nepalis suffered violence and eviction.[lxxxix]

Internally displaced in central India- In central India, leftist extremist groups commonly referred to as Maoists or Naxalites, have significantly increased insurgent activities during the past few years, including in the states of Madhya Pradesh, West Bengal, Bihar, Chhattisgarh, Jharkhand, Orissa, Tamil Nadu, Maharashtra and Andhra Pradesh. Violence has been especially on the increase in Andhra Pradesh and Orissa.[xc] Violence has been especially on the increase in Andhra Pradesh and Orissa.[xci] Distinction against the tribal population, displacement by large development projects and government failure to ensure food security have been the main reasons for the rapid spread of the Naxalite movement, according to an independent study released in June 2005.[xcii] No estimate of the number of people Displaced as a result of the insurgency in central India is available, but anecdotal information suggests that thousands of villagers have been Displaced either as a result of government mobilization against the insurgent groups or because they flee Naxalite violence. In Chhattisgarh, approximately 15,000 people from 420 villages have fled to temporary camps. People have left behind their cattle and most of their household goods. Displacement is reportedly continuing while more police and para-military stations are being set up. 7,000– 10,000 people fled to camps protected by the police to avoid Naxalite retaliation because they had joined the Salva Jodum movement. In Orissa, the state authorities have reportedly forcibly displaced local tribes because they were suspected of sympathizing with the Naxalites.[xciii]

b) Displacement due to Development- Dam building is one of the most important causes for development related displacement. According to a report, 'during the last fifty years, some 3,300 big dams have been constructed in India. Many of them have led to large-scale forced eviction of vulnerable groups. The situation of the tribal people is of special concern as they constitute 40 to 50 percent of the displaced population'. The brutality of displacement due to the building of dams was dramatically highlighted during the agitation over the Sardar Sarovar Dam. It has been called 'India's most controversial dam project'. Medha Patekar, spearhead the anti-dam movement known as the Narmada Bachao Andolon. This movement for the first time systematically revealed how building dams can result in total dislocation of tribal societies. The beneficiaries of the dam are meant to be large landowners; but the tribal people are paying the price. The Narmada Valley Development Project (NVDP) is supposed to be the most ambitious river valley development project in the world. It envisages building 3,200 dams that would reconstitute the Narmada and her 419 tributaries into a series of step-reservoirs. Of these, 30 would be major dams, 135 medium and the rest small. Two of the major dams would be multi-purpose mega dams. The Sardar Sarovar in Gujarat and the Narmada Sagar in Madhya Pradesh, would, between them, hold more water than any other reservoir in the Indian subcontinent. The official figure indicates that about 42,000 families would be displaced but non-governmental organizations such as the Narmada Bachao Andolan (NBA) puts the figure to about 85,000 families or 500,000 people. They argue that the official figure has not counted people who would lose their livelihood as a result of these dams as 'Project Affected Families' (PAFs). The official figure counts families who would lose their land or homes as the only PAF. The Narmada Valley Development Project would affect the lives of 25 million people who would in the valley and would alter the ecology of an entire river basin.

The Tehri project is a multi-purpose irrigation and power project in the Ganges valley, 250 km north of Delhi, located in the Tehri Garhwal district of Uttaranchal state. Initially in 1969, the Tehri Dam Project Organization (TDPO) estimated that about 13,413 persons would be affected by the construction of the dam. But a working group for the Environment Appraisal of Tehri Dam established in 1979 put the figure of expected internal displacement to 85,600 persons. According to the 1995 report of TDPO, out of 135 villages affected, 37 would be fully submerged once the dam is completed. The total land affected by the project is 13,000 hectares. Dams are built, people are uprooted, forests are submerged and then the project is simply abandoned. Canals are never completed, the benefits never accrue. The first dam that was built on the Narmada is a case in point - the Bargi Dam in Madhya Pradesh was completed in 1990. It cost ten times more than was budgeted and submerged three times more land than engineers said it would. To save the cost and effort of doing a survey, the government just filled the reservoir without warning anybody. 70,000 people from 101 villages were supposed to be displaced. Instead, 114,000 people from 162 villages were displaced. They were evicted from their homes by rising waters, chased out like rats, with no prior notice. There was no rehabilitation. Some got meager cash compensation. Most got nothing. Some died of starvation. Others moved to slums in Jabalpur. Today, ten years after it was completed, the Bargi Dam produces some electricity, but irrigates only as much land as it submerged. Only 5 per cent of the land its planners claimed it would irrigate. Tribal people are more dependent on forest and common property resources than other groups. Fewer tribal than non-tribal are being properly resettled or get benefits from the project displacing them. Landless agricultural workers generally do not receive any compensation. Tribal people share the problems of other rural people but they are even more dependent on forests and common property resources, their documented legal rights on cultivable lands are even more tenuous, their ability to handle.[xciv]

Judicial Approach

There are certain times where the subject matter which will cause displacement of people at large has been taken to the court. In *Banbasi Seva Ashram v. State of Uttar Pradesh*[xcv] National Thermal Power Cooperation Limited (NTPC) decided to set up a thermal plant on the part of the land which would evict the people residing over that place for years. When the matter was taken to the court gave comprehensive directions for rehabilitation of adivasis/landholders affected by the Rihand Super Thermal Power Project to be set up by NTPC and appointed Board of Commissioners to supervise the implementation of directions given by the court. In order to ensure that the rights of the ousters are determined in their respective holdings and they are properly and adequately compensated, the NTPC shall take, in collaboration with the State Government, should take measures as directed by the court in actual physical possession of the lands/houses etc. In, *Gramin Seva Sanstha v. State of Madhya Pradesh*[xcvi] the Madhya Pradesh Legislature enacted the Madhya Pradesh Project Displaced Persons (Resettlement) Act 1985 but unfortunately, the Hasdeo Bango Dam Project has not been brought under the coverage of this Act. As a result there is was no statutory obligation on the Madhya Pradesh Government to provide resettlement and rehabilitation of the large number of tribes who will be uprooted as a result of implementation of this Project. If the object and purpose of the Act is to provide resettlement and rehabilitation to the tribes who were uprooted as a result of which projects being undertaken by the State Government., it is difficult to see why this large project of Hasdeo Bango Dam had not been brought within the Act. Later it was decided that compensation will be given to the people who were displaced due to the occurrence of the dam.

Concusion

Internal displacement remains is most significant human rights and humanitarian challenges for the Nation. The world's Internally Displaced Persons population outnumbers the global refugee population. Thus it can be well derived that there is a need of special and immediate attention for the Internally Displaced

In India, the conditions of the Internally Displaced Persons are not good. The court directs compensation as well as for resettlement and rehabilitation for Internally Displaced Persons. Indiad is a developing country and is already struggling with overpopulation. India is the 2nd most populated country in the world with over 1.21 billion people as per according 2011 census. Population dencity is high in most of the areas. The addition of displaced persons also make the condition of the areas where they arrive pathetic. At many occasions a conflict between the people living in a particular territory and the internally displaced persons who are settled there are clearly visible. These are the conflicts of interests, the clash of habitat, livelihood etc. It poses a challenge to the law and order situations as the crime rate, theft, rape, prostitution etc also gets increased in such areas. The government and the non governmental organizations have to be extra careful in preventing such painful situations.

Essay –V

SEXUAL HARASSMENT OF WOMEN AT WORKPLACE

Introduction

As per the universal understanding of the human rights, all human beings are free and equal in dignity and rights. This has also got reflected in the Universal Declaration of Human Rights. But the irony is that violence against women is a manifestation of historically unequal power equations between men and women. This is a result of domination over and discrimination against women by men.

From the ancient times women have been participating shoulder to shoulder with the male counterparts in earning the livelihood for the family. They used to work in the fields day and night. With industrialization they started working in the factories also .Today women are capable to work in the different capacity in diverse areas like education, health, industry, art, science and technology, police, defense, media and all other fields. But it's a bitter fact that violence against working women is widespread in almost all the service sectors, both developed and developing countries. Physical and emotional abuse of working women is common in all parts of the world.

No matter how hard we try to protect abused women by passing laws, it is still the most common kind of violence against women. In our male dominated society working women are all over the workplaces, being harassed and tortured. It is happening in rural areas, towns, cities and in metropolitans all the places.

The women who does not work outside the home are definitely not "*non-workers*" as their labour could also be converted into money but their labour is not recognised in the male dominated Indian patriarchal system. Women in employment not only develops her independence and personality but she also becomes an asset to her family and the society. Thus the economically empowered women are able to contribute in a better manner towards the development of the society and the Country as a whole. Gender equality in the sphere of employment builds an amicable and safe environment for women to work at ease and to give the benefit of her qualities to the society. Therefore it is all the more important to provide a safe working environment to the women.

Robert Ingersoll, had also commented once that, "There will never be a generation of great men until there has been a generation of free women-of free mind". According to The Centre for Enquiry into Health and Allied Themes (CEHAT), in India" social norms and cultural practices are deep rooted in a highly patriarchal social order where women are expected to adhere to strict gender roles about what they can and cannot do. Women are subject to double discrimination, being members of a specific caste, class or ethnic group, apart from experiencing gendered vulnerabilities. Now to add on to this, the areas in which the women are employed have become another ground to harass them. For example the women who work till late night of in the night shift are looked upon with suspicion and ridicule. Similarly the women who work in fashion or entertainment industry are often subjected to suspicion of having low moral values.

Unfortunately, working women are on the one hand stressed by their responsibilities at the home front on the other hand they fall prey to the acts of harassment at workplace.

International Framework

The struggle for the protection of rights of working women has got impetus through the efforts of various women's groups and non-governmental organizations. After the framing of the Universal Declaration of Human Rights, the rights of working women against exploitation have got recognized as a basic human rights.

Protection has been given through the United Nations' General Assembly

Resolution on the Declaration on the Elimination of Violence Against Women defines violence against women to include sexual harassment, which is prohibited at work, in educational institutions, and elsewhere (Art. 2(b)), and development of penal, civil or other administrative sanctions, as well as preventative approaches to eliminate violence against women (Art. 4(d-f)). The Convention on the Elimination of all Forms of Discrimination against Women (CEDAW), 1979 directs States Parties to take appropriate measures to eliminate discrimination against women in all fields, specifically including equality under law, in governance and politics, the workplace, education, healthcare, and in other areas of public and social life. (Arts. 7-16). CEDAW, 1979, is the United Nations' landmark treaty marking the struggle for women's right. It is regarded as the Bill of Rights for women. It graphically puts what constitutes discrimination against women and spells out tools so that women's rights are not violated and they are conferred the same rights. CEDAW was ratified by the UNO on 18-12-1979 and the Government of India had ratified as an active participant on 19-6-1993 acceded to CEDAW and reiterated that discrimination against women violates the principles of equality of rights and respect for human dignity and it is an obstacle to the participation on equal terms with men in the political, social, economic and cultural life of their country; it hampers the growth of the personality from society and family, making more difficult for the full development of potentialities of women in the service of the respective countries and of humanity.[xcvii]

The equality principles were reaffirmed in the Second World Conference on Human Rights at Vienna in June 1993 and in the Fourth World Conference on Women held in Beijing in 1995. India was a party to this Convention and other Declarations and is committed to actualize them. In 1993 Conference, gender-based violence and all categories of sexual harassment and exploitation were condemned. A part of the Resolution reads thus:

The human rights of women and of the girl child are an inalienable, integral and indivisible part of universal human rights. The World Conference on Human Rights urges governments, institutions, intergovernmental and non-governmental organizations to intensify their efforts for the protection of human rights of women and the girl child.

The other relevant International Instruments on Women are: (i) Convention on the Political Rights of Women (1952), (ii) International Covenant on Civil and Political Rights (1966), (iii) International Covenant on Economic, Social and Cultural Rights (1966), (iv) Declaration on the Elimination of All Forms of Discrimination against Women (1967), (v) Declaration on the Protection of Women and Children in Emergency and Armed Conflict (1974), (vi) Inter-American Convention for the Prevention,

Punishment and Elimination of Violence against Women (1995), (vii) Universal Declaration on Democracy (1997), and (viii) Optional Protocol to the Convention on the Elimination of All Forms of Discrimination against Women (1999).

The ILO Committee of Experts on the Application of Conventions and Recommendations has confirmed that sexual harassment is a form of sex discrimination covered by the Discrimination (Employment and Occupation) Convention (No. 111) of 1958. The ILO's Indigenous and Tribal Peoples Convention (No. 169) also specifically prohibits sexual harassment in the workplace.

Human Rights of Women and the Constitution of India

The Constitution of India is true guarantor of right of equality of women. It is a fundamental document which deals with women's right to Equality in India. Which is the first condition of economic empowerment. Further the Constitution of India provide special protection to women with the help of various provisions inserted under Part III. Article 14 confers the equality before law or the equal protection of the law to every person. Article 15(1) prohibits any discrimination on grounds of religion, race, sex, or place of birth. 15(3) empower the state to make any special provision for women and children. Article 16 guarantees equality of opportunity for all citizens in matters relating to employment or opportunity to any office under the state and forbids the discrimination on the grounds only of inter alia sex. Article 19 guarantees the two important freedoms:

(a) Freedom of speech and expression - Art. 19(1) (a); and

(b) Freedom to practice any profession or to carry out any occupation, trade or business - Art. 19(1) (g). Article 21 ensures; 'no person shall be deprived of his life or personal liberty except according to procedure established by law'. Women have a right to lead a dignified, honourable and peaceful life with liberty.

Part IV of the Constitution of India deals with Directive Principles of State Policy. Article 39[xcviii] in Part IV of the Constitution that deals with Directive Principles of State Policy, provides that the State shall direct its policies towards securing that the citizens, men and women equally, have the right to adequate means of livelihood. Clause (d) of the said Article provides for equal pay for equal work for both men and women and Clause (e) stipulates that health and strength of workers, men and women, and the tender age of children are not abused and that citizens are not forced by economic necessity to enter into avocations unsuited to their age or strength.

The Article 51-A (Fundamental Duties) Clauses (e) and (j) and provide as follows:

(e) to promote harmony and the spirit of common brotherhood amongst all the people of India transcending religious, linguistic and regional or sectional diversities; to renounce practices derogatory to the dignity of women; are to be renounced. Be it stated, dignity is the quintessential quality of a personality and a human frames always desires to live in the mansion of dignity, for it is a highly cherished value. Clause (j) has to be understood in the backdrop that India is a welfare State and, therefore, it is the duty of the State to promote justice, to provide equal opportunity to see that all citizens and they are not deprived of by reasons of economic disparity. It is also the duty of the State to frame policies so that men and women have the right to adequate means of livelihood. It is also the duty of the citizen to strive towards excellence in all spheres of individual and collective activity so that the nation constantly rises to higher levels of endeavour and achievement. Besides, the constitutional framework Indian Parliament has also framed various legislations to protect women's rights

Judicial Response

The public at large have faith in our Judiciary. The Supreme Court is the final interpreter of the Constitution of India. The judiciary is the protector of Human Rights over decades. The initiative of Judiciary has been shown in its various verdicts. The Supreme Court of India has interpreted various provisions of international instruments correlated with Constitutional law of India. India is a signatory to various International Conventions and Treaties. The Universal Declaration of Human Rights adopted on 10th Dec. 1948, has greatly helped to create a universal thinking that Human Rights are supreme shall preserve.

Mrs. Neera Mathur v. Life Insurance Corporation of India and Anr.[xcix], a female candidate was required to furnish information about her menstrual period, last date of menstruation, pregnancy and miscarriage. The Court declared that calling of such information are indeed embarrassing if not humiliating. The Court directed that the employer i.e. Life Insurance Corporation would do well to delete such columns in the declaration.

In *Rupan Deol Bajaj Vs. K.P.S.Gill*,[c] a senior IAS officer, Rupan Deol Bajaj was slapped on the posterior by the then Chief of Police, Punjab, Mr. K.P.S.Gill at a dinner party in July 1988. Rupan Bajaj filed a suit against him, despite the public opinion that she was blowing it out of proportion, along with the attempts by all the senior officials of the state to suppress the matter. The Supreme Court in January, 1998 fined Mr.K.P.S.Gill Rs.2.5 lacs in lieu of three months rigorous imprisonment under Sections. 294 and 509 of the Indian Penal Code.

In *N. Radhabai Vs. D. Ramchandran*, when Radhabai, Secretary to D. Ramchandran, the then social minister for state protested against his abuse of girls in the welfare institutions, he attempted to molest her, which was followed by her dismissal. The Supreme Court in 1995 passed the judgment in her favour, with back pay and perks from the date of dismissal.

In *Valsamma Paul (Mrs) v. Cochin University*[ci] The Supreme Court has observed that the human rights are derived from the dignity and worth inherent in the human person. Human rights and fundamental freedoms have been reiterated in the Universal Declaration of Human Rights. Democracy, development and respect for human rights and fundamental freedoms are interdependent and have mutual reinforcement. The human rights for women, including girl child are, therefore, inalienable, integral and an indivisible part of universal human rights. The full development of personality and fundamental freedoms and equal participation by women in political, social, economic and cultural life are concomitants for national development, social and family stability and growth--cultural, social and economical. All forms of discrimination on grounds of gender is violative of fundamental freedoms and human rights... On a perusal of the Articles of the aforesaid Convention(CEDAW), it is clear as crystal that apart from right to work being an inalienable right of all human beings, it has commended the right to same employment opportunity, including the application of same criteria for selection in matters of employment and all steps to be taken to eliminate discrimination against women in the field of employment in order to ensure equality among man and women. It is founded on social security and many other facets.
It was in *Vishaka Vs. State of Rajasthan*[cii], that for the first time sexual harassment had been explicitly- legally defined as an unwelcome sexual gesture or behaviour whether made directly or indirectly.

The Court referred to the 1993 Treaty and opined that the meaning and content of Fundamental Rights in the Constitution are of sufficient amplitude to encompass all the facets of gender equality including prevention of sexual harassment or abuse. In that context, the Court observed thus:

"The international conventions and norms are to be read into them in the absence of enacted domestic law occupying the fields when there is no inconsistency between them. It is now an accepted rule of judicial construction that regard must be had to international conventions and norms fro construing domestic law when there is no inconsistency between them and there is a void in the domestic law.

The three-Judge Bench, while noting the increasing awareness on gender justice, took note of the increase in the effort to guard against such violations. The Court observed that when there is violation of gender justice and working women is sexually harassed, there is violation of the fundamental rights of gender justice and it is clear violation of the rights Under Articles 14, 15 and 21 of the Constitution

In the abovementioned case, the judgment was delivered by J.S.Verma. CJ, on behalf of Sujata Manohar and B.N.Kirpal, JJ., on a writ petition filed by 'Vihska'- a non Governmental organization working for gender equality by way of PIL seeking enforcement of fundamental rights of working women under Article.21 of the Constitution.

The immediate cause for filing the petition was the alleged brutal gang rape of a social worker of Rajasthan. The Supreme Court in absence of any enacted law (which still remains absent- save the Supreme Court guidelines as stated hereunder) to provide for effective enforcement of basic human rights of gender equality and guarantee against sexual harassment, laid down the following guidelines:

1. All the employers in charge of work place whether in the public or the private sector, should take appropriate steps to prevent sexual harassment without prejudice to the generality of his obligation, he should take the following steps:

a) Express prohibition of sexual harassment which includes physical contact and advances, a demand or request for sexual favours, sexually coloured remarks, showing pornographic or any other unwelcome physical, verbal/non-verbal conduct of sexual nature should be noticed, published and circulated in appropriate ways.

    b) The rules and regulations of government and public sector bodies relating to conduct and discipline should include rules prohibiting sexual harassment and provide for appropriate penalties in such rules against the offender.

    c) As regards private employers, steps should be taken to include the aforesaid prohibitions in the Standing Orders under the Industrial Employment (Standing Orders) Act, 1946.

    d) Appropriate work conditions should be provided in respect of work leisure, health, hygiene- to further ensure that there is no hostile environment towards women and no woman should have reasonable grounds to believe that she is disadvantaged in connection with her employment.

2. Where such conduct amounts to specific offences under the Indian Penal Code or any other law the employer shall initiate appropriate action in accordance with the law, by making a complaint with the appropriate authority.

3. Victims of sexual harassment should have the option to seek transfer of the perpetrator or their own transfer.

In Apparel Export Promotion Council, Appellant v. *A.K. Chopra*[iii] case, is the first case in which the Supreme Court applied the law laid down in Vishaka's case and upheld the dismissal of a superior officer of the Delhi based Apparel Export Promotion Council who was found guilty of sexual harassment of a subordinate female employee at the place of work on the ground that it violated her fundamental right guaranteed by Article 21 of the Constitution.

In both cases the Supreme Court observed, that " *In cases involving Human Rights, the Courts must be alive to the International Conventions and Instruments as far as possible to give effect to the principles contained therein- such as the Convention on the Eradication of All forms of Discrimination Against Women, 1979 [CEDAW] and the Beijing Declaration directing all state parties to take appropriate measures to prevent such discrimination.*"

The guidelines and judgments have identified sexual harassment as a question of power exerted by the perpetrator on the victim. Therefore sexual harassment in addition to being a violation of the right to safe working conditions, is also a violation of the right to bodily integrity of the woman.

The Legal Framework:

Earlier there were no specific laws which could deals with the cases of sexual harassment. Before 1997, women experiencing sexual harassment at workplace had to lodge a complaint under Section 354 of the Indian Penal Code that deals with the 'criminal assault of women to outrage women's modesty', and Section 509 that punishes an individual/individuals for using a 'word, gesture or act intended to insult the modesty of a woman'. Until the making of legal framework the Guidelines of Vishaka judgment had the effect of law and the Guidelines were to be mandatorily followed by organizations, both in the private and government sector.

While there were several attempts made to enact a law on this subject previously, the Sexual Harassment of Women at Workplace (Prevention,

Prohibition and Redressal) Bill, 2012 was eventually passed by the Lower House of the Parliament (Lok Sabha) on September 3, 2012, then passed by the Upper House of the Parliament (Rajya Sabha) on February 26, 2013 and received the President's assent on April 22, 2013.

The Sexual Harassment of Women at Workplace (Prevention, Prohibition and Redressal) Act, 2013-

This is an Act to provide protection against sexual harassment of women at workplace and for the Prevention and Redressal of complaints of sexual harassment and for matters connected therewith or incidental thereto. The preamble states that sexual harassment results in violation of the fundamental rights of a woman to equality under articles 14 and 15 of the Constitution of India and her right to life and to live with dignity under article 21 of the Constitution and right to practice any profession or to carry on any occupation, trade or business which includes a right to a safe environment free from sexual harassment.The enactment has provisions for giving effect to CEDAW for protection of women against sexual harassment at workplace.

The 2013 Sexual Harassment Act provides that sexual harassment constitutes of the following unwelcome acts or behavior (whether directly or by implication) namely:

(i) physical contact and advances; or

(ii) a demand or request for sexual favors; or

(iii) making sexually colored remarks; or

(iv) showing pornography; or

(v) any other unwelcome physical, verbal or non-verbal conduct of sexual nature.

Further on, the act states that the following circumstances, along other circumstances, if they occur or are in relation to or connected with any act or behavior of sexual harassment may amount to sexual harassment:-

(i) implied or explicit promise of preferential treatment in her employment.

(ii) implied or explicit threat of detrimental treatment in her employment

(iii)   implied or explicit threat about her present or future employment

(iv)   interferes with her work or creating an intimidating or offensive work environment for her; or

(v)   humiliating treatment likely to affect her health or safety

The Act defines sexual harassment at the work place and creates a mechanism for redressal of complaints. It also provides safeguards against false or malicious charges. The definition of "aggrieved woman", who will get protection under the Act is extremely wide to cover all women, irrespective of her age or employment status, whether in the organised or unorganised sectors, public or private and covers clients, customers and domestic workers as well. While the "workplace" in the Vishaka guidelines is confined to the traditional office set-up where there is a clear employer-employee relationship, the Act goes much further to include organisations, department, office, branch unit etc. in the public and private sector, organized and unorganized, hospitals, nursing homes, educational institutions, sports institutes, stadiums, sports complex and any place visited by the employee during the course of employment including the transportation. The Committee is required to complete the inquiry within a time period of 90 days. On completion of the inquiry, the report will be sent to the employer or the District Officer, as the case may be, they are mandated to take action on the report within 60 days.

Every employer is required to constitute an Internal Complaints Committee at each office or branch with 10 or more employees. The District Officer is required to constitute a Local Complaints Committee at each district, and if required at the block level.

The Complaints Committees have the powers of civil courts for gathering evidence. The Complaints Committees are required to provide for conciliation before initiating an inquiry, if requested by the complainant. Penalties have been prescribed for employers. Non-compliance with the provisions of the Act shall be punishable with a fine of up to ₹ 50,000. Repeated violations may lead to higher penalties and cancellation of licence or registration to conduct business.

The Deadlock

The section 14 of the Act provides makes provision for punishment clause for filing of false and malicious complaint by the complainant against the Respondent' as if the section prevail under the Act then this will deter the women to come forward and file even the genuine cases. Section 14 provides:-

"(i)Where the Internal Committee or the Local Committee, as the case may be arrives at a conclusion that the allegation against the respondent is false or malicious or the aggrieved woman or any other person making the complaint has produced any forged or misleading document, it may recommend to the employer or the District Officer, as the case may be, to take action against the woman or the person who has made the complaint under sub-section (1) or sub-section (2) of section 9, as the case may be, in accordance with the provisions of the service rules applicable to her or him or where no such service rules exist, in such manner as may be prescribed:

Provided that a mere inability to substantiate a complaint or provide adequate proof need not attract action against the complainant under this section:

Provided further that the malicious intent or falsehood on part of the complaint shall be established after an inquiry in accordance with the procedure prescribed, before any action is recommended.

(2) Where the Internal Committee or the Local Committee, as the case may be, arrives at a conclusion that during the inquiry any witness has given false evidence or produced any forged or misleading document, it may recommend to the employer of the witness or the District Officer, as the case may be to take action in accordance with the provisions of the service rules applicable to the said witness or where no such service rules exist, in such manner as may be prescribed."

Upon the Act's presidential approval, section was added to the Indian Penal Code,1860 that stipulates what consists of a sexual harassment offence and what the penalties shall be for a man committing such an offence. Penalties range from one to three years imprisonment and/or a fine. Additionally, with sexual harassment being a crime, employers are obligated report offences.

Conclusion

The enforcement of The Sexual Harassment of Women at Workplace (Prevention, Prohibition and Redressal) Act, 2013 has is a major breakthrough in the area of women's rights. The Act is elaborately covering the different kinds of sexual harassment of women at workplace and containing provisions to protect the women. The only weakness of the Act is section 14.

The danger involved here is that the entire purpose of Vishakha and this law might be defeated. Complaint 'not proved' does not mean that the complaint is false. There are remedies under the ordinary law (e.g. defamation) to resort to if the complaint is found to be 'false'. Another question that arises is that how the members of complaints committee shall measure if complaints are made 'maliciously'. Most complainants approach inquiry committees tentatively in the first place, given that acts of sexual harassment usually happen behind closed doors, without witnesses. Aggrieved women will quite naturally evaluate their own complaints as ones that can be judged as false or motivated. Most women, even if they do report a case, quickly become isolated at the workplace without support to prove their case. So in such an environment, the women have to deal with the provision of being penalised in case a complaint is not proved.

Therefore section 14 could be a hindrance to the Act. Though passing the Bill is an important step towards filling the gap, it provides for an action against the complainant in case of a false or malicious complaint. The threat of punitive action for false complaints will definitely act as an obstacle. There is a possibility that not many women approach the police to register a complaint due to this provision.

Essay-VI

SEXUAL OFFENCE AGAINST WOMEN

Violence against women has become phenomenon in the country like India. Women suffer from such violence at various stages of her life from cradle to grave. Some cases are reported many remain confined behind the closed doors of home due to shame and social pressures. Sexual offences are the most heinous offences against humanity. The victim of rape and other kinds of such offences not only suffers from physical pain but lot of emotional loss is suffered by her. Along with that social stigma and sense of shame is also subjected to such victims.

As a result of demand from the women's rights organizations and the pressure due to increasing violence against women,On 22 December 2012, a judicial committee headed by J. S. Verma, a former Chief Justice of India, was appointed by the Central government to submit a report, within 30 days, to suggest amendments to criminal law to sternly deal with sexual assault cases. The Committee submitted its report after 29 days on 23 January 2013, after considering 80,000 suggestions received by them during the period from public in general and particularly eminent jurists, legal professionals, NGOs, women's groups and civil society, non governmental organizations etc.. The Justice Verma Committee (JVC) report was a landmark statement, applauded by all citizens, welcomed by all Political Parties. JVC was significant because it showed a mirror to the Constitution of India, and reflected its wise and just guarantees of women's equality. The report indicated that failures on the part of the Government and Police were the root cause behind crimes against women. Major suggestions of the report included the need to review maximum punishment for rape as life imprisonment and not death penalty, clear ambiguity over control of Delhi Police etc. The JVC report recommends that age of consent be retained at 16 years as it always has been in the IPC, to prevent criminalization of young persons for consensual sex. Women's groups are merely asking for it to be retained at 16 years, rather than increase it unthinkingly to 18 years. The report also suggested for the criminalization of rape in marriage, and amending Armed Forces (Special Powers) Act so that no sanction is needed for prosecuting an armed force personnel accused of a crime against woman. The Cabinet Ministers on 1 February 2013 approved for bringing an ordinance, for giving effect to the changes in law as suggested by the Verma Committee Report. According to former, Minister of Law and Justice, Ashwani Kumar, 90 percent of the suggestions given by the Verma Committee Report had been incorporated into the Ordinance.

An Ordinance was promulgated by the President of India, Pranab Mukherjee, on 3 February 2013, in light of the protests in the 2012 Delhi gang rape case, the incident generated international coverage and was condemned by the United Nations Entity for Gender Equality and the Empowerment of Women, who called on the Government of India and the Government of Delhi "to do everything in their power to take up radical reforms, ensure justice and reach out with robust public services to make women's lives more safe and secure".

Afterwards, in order to make the criminal law more effective certain major amendments have been done in the Indian Penal Code, 1980. These changes were carried out by the Criminal Law (Amendment Act). The Criminal Law (Amendment) Act, 2013 is an Indian legislation passed by the Lok Sabha on 19 March 2013, and by the Rajya Sabha on 21 March 2013, which provides for amendment of Indian Penal Code, Indian Evidence Act, and Code of Criminal Procedure, 1973, Protection of children from sexual offences Act 2012. The Bill received Presidential assent on 2 April 2013 and deemed to have come into force from 3rd day of February 2013.

The new Act has expressly recognised certain acts as offences which were dealt under related laws. These new offences like, acid attack, sexual harassment, voyeurism, stalking have been incorporated into the Indian Penal Code. By the new added seventh clause to the section 100 of IPC the right of private defence of the body extends to causing death against an Act throwing or administering acid or an attempt to throw or administer acid which may reasonably cause the apprehension that grievous hurt will otherwise be the consequence of such act .The punishment for acid attack has been inserted by Sec. 326 A as imprisonment for a term which shall not be less than 10 years and extends to life imprisonment to the perpetrators who caused permanent, partial disability or deformity or grievous hurt to the victim with the fine which is reasonable to meet the medical expenses of the treatment of the victim. By inserting Sec.326.B the attempt to acid attack has also made punishable with not less than 5 years imprisonment which may extend to 7 years.[civ] This provision is of great relevance at the instance of increasing acid attacks against the woman in the country. Acid attacks in India, have a gendered aspect to them: analyses of news reports revealed at least 72% of reported attacks involved women. From January 2002 to October 2010, 153 cases of acid assault were reported in Indian print media, while 174 judicial cases were reported for the year of 2000. However, scholars think that this is an underestimation, given that not all attacks are reported in the news, nor do all victims report the crime to officials. The motivation for acid attacks in India, the 34% of the analyzed print media in India cited rejection of marriage or refusal by women of sexual advances as the cause of the attack and dowry disagreements have been shown to spur acid attacks. Land, property, and/or business disputes accounted for 20% of acid assaults in India from 2002 to 2010. The incident Sonali Mukherjee's case where the perpetrators were granted bail after being sentenced to nine years of Jail. Thereafter, when her family approached High Court, all the legislators, and MPs in search of justice, all she got in return was assurances and "nothing else". The perpetrators got away scot-free. Without media attention, an acid attack victim languishes in pain and poverty, their families often unable to bear the medical expenses.

Various forceful changes have resulted in the legislations by the amendments. The Criminal Law (Amendment) Act has made the assault or criminal force to woman with intent to outrage her modesty punishable with imprisonment for either description for a term which shall not be less than one year but which may extend to five years, and shall also be liable to fine.

Subjoining of sections 354A (1) (1-iv), (2) (3) to the Sec. 354 of Indian Penal Code triggers various unwanted acts against womanhood punishable. Sexual harassment which includes physical contact and advances involving unwelcome and explicit sexual overtures, or a demand or request for sexual favours, showing pornography against the will of a woman, has been made punishable with imprisonment [cv] which may extend to three years with fine or both and making sexually coloured remarks which shall be punished with imprisonment which may extend to one year with fine or both.

By the new Act any man who assaults or uses criminal forces to any woman or abets such act with the intention of disrobing or compelling her to be naked, shall be punished with imprisonment of either description for a term which shall not be less than three years but which may extend to seven years, and shall also be liable to fine.

Voyeurism which is common and curtails the privacy of a woman got a new dimension by the approach on the new Act. This new approach is a great relief for the Indian womanhood. By the new provision any man who watches, or captures the image of a woman engaging in a private act in circumstances where she would usually have the expectation of not being observed either by the perpetrator or by any other person at the behest of the perpetrator or disseminates such image shall be punished on first conviction with imprisonment of either description for a term which shall not be less than one year but which may extend to three years and shall also be liable to fine and be punished on a second or subsequent conviction with imprisonment of either description for a term which shall not be less than three but which may extend to seven years, and shall also be liable to fine.

Sec. 7, Criminal Law Amendment Act, 2013 ,Sec. 354B Indian Penal Code - 7 Sec. 354C Stalking- A man will be punishable for imprisonment which may extend to 3 years and 5 years for first and second conviction respectively , who follows a woman and contacts or attempts to contact such woman to foster personal interaction repeatedly despite a clear indication of disinterest by such woman: or monitors the use by a woman of the internet, email or any other form of electronic communication. The recent upswing in cases of molestation and stalking at the JNU Delhi premise, have also drawn attention in the Indian society recently.

Rape- In the case of rape which can be considered as the most brutal crime against the womanhood the new amendment Act has wided the range of acts that will constitute the crime of rape. The punishment to rape under the new Act is the rigourous imprisonment not less than 7 years but which may extend to life imprisonment10 and in several instances or by particular persons those who has identified as perpetrators then the imprisonment which shall not be less than 10 years as well and imprisonment till the end of remaining natural life with fine. If the rape has caused death or permanent vegitative stage of the victim then the punishment is rigourous imprisonment which shall not be less than 20 years and imprisonment of life which shall mean imprisonment for the remainder of the culprits natural life or death which is the maximum punishment established by the Indian Penal System.

By the Amendment Act the offence which does not amount to rape but inducing or seducing a woman to have sexual intercourse by abusing the position of authority is also made punishable for rigourous imprisonment which is not less than 5 years but may extend to 10 years. In the case of gang rape the punishment extends for a term not less than 20 years but which may extend to life which may extend to imprisonment for the remainder of that person's natural life, and with fine which is reasonable for the medical expenses and rehabilitation of the victim.

The punishment for repeat offenders leads to imprisonment for the remainder of that person's natural life, and with death. Rape and murder of Software engineer Nayana Pujari by an escort driver in Pune in 2009, The gang rape of a 23-year old student on a public bus, are the two representative victims of rape crimes which largely taking place all over the India. Many of the rape crimes has left out without reporting and the stringent and hardest punishments against rape gives a hope that there will be vanishing of crimes by fear of the punishment. Almost every women in India suffers molestation atleast once in her life. In the most common crime against woman that is of use of Word, Gesture, or act intended to insult the modesty of a woman the punishment has increased to 3 years punishment with fine from the 1 year punishment or with fine or with both which is hopefully will reduce the chance of the common practice of this crime against woman. It is need of the hour that such cases must be reported and speedy trial must be done to punish the offenders because such instances have become very common in almost all the public places whether markets, footpaths, bus stops or in the buses.

Approach of Courts Before the Amendments

Dhananjoy Chaterjee vs State Of W.B[cvi]

Dhananjoy Chatterjee was a security guard, who was executed by hanging for the murder following a rape of 14-year-old Hetal on March 5, 1990 at her apartment residence in Bhowanipur. In the Dhananjoy Chatterjee case, the court had made some very interesting observations pertaining to rape and murder, which will be applicable to the Delhi gangrape case.

The court had said, "In recent years, the rising crime rate, particularly violent crime against women, has made the criminal sentencing by the courts a subject of concern. Today, there are admitted disparities. Some criminals get very harsh sentences while many receive a grossly different sentence for an essentially equivalent crime and a shockingly large number even go unpunished thereby encouraging the criminal and in the ultimate making justice suffer by weakening the system's credibility. Of course, it is not possible to lay down any cut and dry formula relating to imposition of sentence but the object of sentencing should be to see that the crime does not go unpunished and the victim of crime as also the society has the satisfaction that justice has been done to it. In imposing sentences in the absence of specific legislation, judges must consider variety of factors and after considering all those factors and taking an overall view of the situation, impose sentence, which they consider to be an appropriate one. Aggravating factors cannot be ignored and similarly mitigating circumstances have also to be taken into consideration."

"The measure of punishment in a given case must depend upon the atrocity of the crime; the conduct of the criminal and the defenceless and unprotected state of the victim. Imposition of appropriate punishment is the manner in which the courts respond to the society's cry for justice against the criminals. Justice demands that courts should impose punishment befitting the crime so that the courts reflect public abhorrence of the crime. The courts must not only keep in view the rights of the criminal but also the rights of the victim of the crime and the society at large while considering imposition of appropriate punishment," it had said.

"The offence was not only inhuman and barbaric but it was a totally ruthless crime of rape followed by cold-blooded murder and an affront to the human dignity of the society. The savage nature of the crime has shocked our judicial conscience. We agree that a real and abiding concern for the dignity of human life is required to be kept in mind by the courts while considering the confirmation of the sentence of death but a cold blooded preplanned brutal murder, without any provocation, after committing rape on an innocent certainly makes this case a "rarest of the rare" cases which calls for no punishment other than the capital punishment," the court had said.

State vs Jasbir Singh alias Billa And Kuljeet[vii]

Popularly known as the Ranga-Billa Kidnapping Case, was a notorious crime in New Delhi in 1978. Two children, Geeta and Sanjay Chopra, were kidnapped by two young men, Ranga Khus (Kuljeet Singh) and Billa (Jasbir Singh), who planned to demand ransom from their parents. Their plans went awry when their car was involved in a traffic accident with a public bus. They subsequently raped Geeta, murdered the children and fled the city. They were arrested on a train a few months later, tried and hanged for the crime in 1982. The children were reported missing on 26 August 1978 and their bodies discovered on 29 August 1978. Medical examination confirmed that Geeta was raped. It later transpired that they had been kidnapped while hitching a ride from outside Gol Dak Khana near Connaught Place. Both culprits were found guilty and sentenced to death. Capital punishment was given to both of them.

Tuka Ram And Anr vs State Of Maharashtra[viii]

Wherein Mathura- a sixteen year old tribal girl was raped by two policemen in the compound of Desai Ganj Police station in Chandrapur district of Maharashtra.Her relatives, who had come to register a complaint, were patiently waiting outside even as the heinous act was being committed in the police station. When her relatives and the assembled crowd threatened to burn down the police chowky, the two guilty policemen, Ganpat and Tukaram, reluctantly agreed to file a panchnama.

The case came for hearing on 1st June, 1974 in the sessions court. The judgment however turned out to be in favour of the accused. Mathura was accused of being a liar. It was stated that since she was 'habituated to sexual intercourse' her consent was voluntary; under the circumstances only sexual intercourse could be proved and not rape.

On appeal the Nagpur bench of the Bombay High Court set aside the judgment of the Sessions Court, and sentenced the accused namely Tukaram and Ganpat to one and five years of rigorous imprisonment respectively. The Court held that passive submission due to fear induced by serious threats could not be construed as consent or willing sexual intercourse. However, the Supreme Court again acquitted the accused policemen. The Supreme Court held that Mathura had raised no alarm; and also that there were no visible marks of injury on her person thereby negating the struggle by her.

The Court in this case failed to comprehend that a helpless resignation in the face of inevitable compulsion or the passive giving in is no consent. However, the Criminal Law Amendment Act, 1983 has made a statutory provision in the face of Section.114 (A) of the Evidence Act, which states that if the victim girl says that she did no consent to the sexual intercourse, the Court shall presume that she did not consent.

The Chairman, Railway Board & Ors vs Mrs. Chandrima Das & Ors[ix]

A practicing Advocate of the Calcutta High Court filed a petition under Article.226 of the Constitution of India against the various railway authorities of the eastern railway claiming compensation for the victim (Smt. Hanufa Khatoon)- a Bangladesh national- who was raped at the Howrah Station, by the railway security men. The High Court awarded Rs.10 lacs as compensation.

An appeal was preferred and it was contended by the state that:

a)   The railway was not liable to pay the compensation to the victim for she was a foreigner.

b) That the remedy for compensation lies in the domain of private law and not public law. i.e. that the victim should have approached the Civil Court for seeking damages; and should have not come to the High Court under Article.226.

Considering the above said contentions, the Supreme Court observed: "Where public functionaries are involved and the matter relates to the violation of fundamental rights or the enforcement of public duties, the remedy would be avoidable under public law. It was more so, when it was not a mere violation of any ordinary right, but the violation of fundamental rights was involved- as the petitioner was a victim of rape, which a violation of fundamental right of every person guaranteed under Article.21 of the Constitution."

The Supreme Court also held that the relief can be granted to the victim for two reasons- firstly, on the ground of domestic jurisprudence based on the Constitutional provisions; and secondly, on the ground of Human Rights Jurisprudence based on the Universal Declaration of Human Rights, 1948 which has international recognition as the 'Moral Code of Conduct'- adopted by the General Assembly of the United Nation.

Apparel Export Promotion Council vs A.K. Chopra & Others[cx]

A K.Chopra's case, is the first case in which the Supreme Court applied the law laid down in Vishaka's case[cxi] and upheld the dismissal of a superior officer of the Delhi based Apparel Export Promotion Council who was found guilty of sexual harassment of a subordinate female employee at the place of work on the ground that it violated her fundamental right guaranteed by Article.21 of the Constitution.

In both cases the Supreme Court observed, that " In cases involving Human Rights, the Courts must be alive to the International Conventions and Instruments as far as possible to give effect to the principles contained therein- such as the Convention on the Eradication of All forms of Discrimination Against Women, 1979 [CE DAW] and the Beijing Declaration directing all state parties to take appropriate measures to prevent such discrimination."

The guidelines and judgments have identified sexual harassment as a question of power exerted by the perpetrator on the victim. Therefore sexual harassment in addition to being a violation of the right to safe working conditions, is also a violation of the right to bodily integrity of the woman.

Bodhisattwa Gautam vs Miss Subhra Chakraborty[cxii]

The Apex Court gave guidelines to deal with complaints regarding rape- The complainants of sexual assault cases should be provided with legal representation. It is important to secure continuity of assistance by ensuring that the same person who looked after the complainant's interests in the police station represent her till the end of the case. Compensation for victims shall be awarded by the court on conviction of the offender and by the Criminal Injuries Compensation Board whether or not a conviction has taken place. The Board will take into account pain, suffering and shock as well as loss of earnings due to pregnancy and the expenses of the child but if this occurred as a result of the rape.

Conclusion

Although Criminal law Amendment Act has revolutionaized the law relating to sexual assaults on Indian women, marital rape is still not an offence in India. Marital Rape refers to unwanted intercourse by a man with his wife obtained by force, threat of force, or physical violence, or when she is unable to give consent. Marital rape could be by the use of force only, a battering rape or a sadistic/obsessive rape. It is a non-consensual act of violent perversion by a husband against the wife where she is physically and sexually abused. Approximations have quoted that every 6 hours; a young married woman is burnt or beaten to death, or driven to suicide from emotional abuse by her husband. The UN Population Fund states that more than 2/3rds of married women in India, aged between 15 to 49 have been beaten, raped or forced to provide sex. The Criminal Law Amendment Act failed to consider the demand for inclusion of marital rape in the Penal Code. Criminal law Amendent Act has given protection to women in cases of rape and other grave assaults but other kinds of gender based discriminations against women were left from its purview. It needs more clarification on many of its provisions.

Essay-VII

HONOUR KILLING

In the ancient Indian society the girls were given freedom to choose their groom, Love marriages were also common. The stories of " Swayamwar"(choosing of the groom) are mentioned in the great epics of India " Ramayana" and " Mahabharata".Even 'Gandharva Vivah"(love marriage by exchanging garlends) was recognized as a legal hindu marriage in the old hindu laws. But in contemporary Indian society the situation has changed. The families and in turn the society has become intolerant. Financial status, caste, religion, region, language atchave become major criteria for the marriages which is resulting in crime of " honour- killing". Honour killing, is a major obstruction to the women's exercise of right to personal liberty ,to choose their life partners.The male head of the patriarchal families and the institutions like 'Khaap Panchayat' are ordering open slaughter of many couples in the name of family or community honour.

On achieving independence, it was believed that India will usher into a Modern National State wherein there will be no place for any kind of exploitation and suppression either in the name of caste, religion, sex or language, wherein feudal practices and values of the past will be substituted by values of egalitarianism. The Founding Fathers, thus, gave India a Constitution committing it to values of Equality, Liability and Fraternity assuring Human dignity.[cxiii]

Everyone has the right to life, liberty and security of the person. Men and women of full age without any limitation due to race, nationality or religion, have the right to marry or to have a family. They are entitled to equal rights as to marriage and its dissolution. Marriage shall be entered into only with the free and full consent of the attending spouses. The family is the natural and fundamental group, unit of society and is entitled to be protected by society and state.[cxiv]

The honour killings have shattered such dreams and are making mockery of Indian Constitution, which has given right to life and personal liberty to every individual. Disturbing news items are coming from several, parts of the country that young men and women who undergo inter-caste/inter-religion marriage are threatened with violence. If the parents of the boy or girl do not approve of such inter-caste or inter-religions marriage the maximum they can do is that they can cut-off social relation with the' son or the daughter, but they cannot give threats or instigate acts of violence. Women who marry a man of their choice moreover take recourse to law, placing themselves outside the traditional scheme; by the public nature of their action, they shame their guardians leading them to resort to violence to restore their honour. Marriage arrangements are delicate and seen to involve serious balancing acts; any disturbance of this balance by a woman refusing a father's choice are considered to affect the father's standing in society.

Honour Crimes Meaning

Honour crimes are acts of violence, usually murder, 'committed by male family members against female family members either or, who are held to have brought dishonor upon the family. The use of word honour for such a dishonourable act and there is nothing honourable in such killings, and in fact they' are nothing but barbaric and shameful acts of murder committed by brutal, feudal minded persons. The loose term honour killing applies to killing of both males and females in cultures[cxv] that practice it. In broader sense, an honour killing is the murder of a family (woman) or clan member by one or more fellow family members, where the murders (potentially the wider community, who are more or less related with victims) believe that the victim has brought dishonor upon the family, clan or community. Thus honour killing is the murder of womenfolk by family members, generally male, who are compelled to remove stains on their family's honour.

Honour killing is the "unlawful killing of a woman for her actual or perceived morally or mentally unclean and impure behaviour".[cxvi] Honour killings are murders by families on family members who are said to have brought shame on the honour and name of family. These are acts in which "a male member of the family kills a female relative for tarnishing the family image". The term is also defined as the purposeful pre-planned murder, generally of a woman, by or at the command of members of her family stimulated by a perception that she has brought shame on the family.[cxvii]

"Honour killings can also be described as extra-judicial punishment of a female relative for assumed sexual and marriage offences. These offences, which are considered as a misdeed or insult, include sexual faithlessness, marrying without the will of parents or having a relationship that the family considers to be inappropriate and rebelling against the tribal and social matrimonial customs. These acts of killing women are justified on the basis that the offence has brought dishonour and shame to family or tribe".[cxviii]

Another report says that "the regime of honour is unforgiving: women on whom suspicion has fallen are not given an opportunity to defend themselves, and family members have no socially acceptable alternative but to remove the stain on their honour by attacking the women. [cxix]

India, even in 21st century, continues to be influenced by the religious and cultural ways of the society. The cultural values are very integral to the Indian society. And the younger generation who challenges the centuries old established norms continues to face the social stigma and take the wrath of society in form of social boycotts and in some cases, honour killing.[cxx] Talking in Indian context, most of the honour crimes take place as a result of inter-caste or inter-religious marriages. The caste system has deep roots in Indian society and any inter-caste, inter-religion or cross-culture marriages, especially after frequent interferences from the Khap Panchayats, are not a welcoming thought.

Constitutional Provisions

The Constitution of India has ample provisions allowing an individual to exercise his/her choice independent of caste, religion or gender and protection from honour related crimes including honour killings. Such killings also violates Articles 14, 15 (1) & (3), 17, 18, 19 and 21 of the Constitution of India. Following are those Constitutional provisions that substantiate this: Honour Killings are cases of homicide and murder which are grave crimes under the Indian Penal Code (IPC). Section 299 and 301 of the IPC, deals with culpable homicide not amounting to murder while Section 300, deals with murder. Honour killing amounts to homicide and murder because the acts are done with the intention of murdering the victims as they have purportedly brought dishonour upon the family. The perpetrators can be punished as per Section 302 of the IPC.

The Indian Majority Act, Section-3, 1857 states that every person domiciled in India shall attain the age of majority on completion of 18 years and not before. Unless a particular personal law specifies otherwise, every person domiciled in India is deemed to have attained majority upon completion of 18 years of age. However, in the case of a minor for whose person or property, or both, a guardian has been appointed or declared by any court of justice before the age of 18 years, and in case of every minor the superintendence of whose property has been alleged by the Court of Wards, age of majority will be 21 years and not 18.

The Act is relevant in cases where the khap panchayats have forcefully separated married couples who are of eligible age to get married. It is a violation of the provisions under this Act. The main reason behind the enactment of the Special Marriage Act, 1954 was to provide a special form of marriage for the people of India and all Indians residing in foreign countries, irrespective of the religion or faith followed by either party, to perform the intended marriage. Scheduled Castes and Scheduled Tribes (Prevention of Atrocities) Act, 1989 was enacted by the Parliament of India, in order to avert atrocities against Scheduled Castes and Scheduled Tribes. The intention of the Act was to help the social inclusion of Dalits into Indian society. It defines acts such as forcing an SC/ST to eat or drink any inedible or obnoxious substance, removing clothes, parading naked or with painted face or body, assaulting, dishonouring and outraging the modesty of an SC/ST woman, sexual exploitation of an SC/ST woman, forcing an SC/ST to leave his or her house or village as punishable. The Act is linked to honour killings because numerous incidents of honour killing are in relation to caste and religion. The Protection of Human Rights (Amendment) Act, 2006 makes the provision for protection of individual rights of human beings and the constitution of a National Human Rights Commission, State Human Rights Commission and Human Rights Courts for better protection of human rights of individuals. The Indian Evidence Act, 1872 makes provision to punish those who conceal facts, either before or at the time of, or after the alleged crime. Article 13 of the Act: Facts relevant when right or custom is in question - Where the question is as to existence of any right or custom, the following facts are relevant: (a) Any transaction by which the right or custom in question was created, claimed modified, recognized, asserted or denied, or which was inconsistent with its existence; (b) Particular instances in which the right or custom was claimed, recognized, or exercised, or in which its exercise was disputed, asserted, or departed from. The Act is relevant to bring to justice those who become victim because of the verdicts issued by the khap panchayats.

International Provisions

India is a signatory to the *United Nations Convention on the Elimination of all forms of Discrimination against Women (CEDAW 1979)* and has also ratified the convention. The provisions of CEDAW can be used to argue that the tradition and practice of punishing individuals for ill informed ideas of dishonouring the family, is essentially institutionalised discrimination against individuals and creates a legally binding obligation for India, as a State party to the convention, to take all measures to end all forms of the practice of honour killing and ensure that all discrimination against women in matters relating to marriage and family relations are eliminated, providing them with the equal right to enter into marriage and to freely choose a spouse and to enter into marriage with their free and full consent as enumerated in Article 16 of the Indian Constitution. This means ensuring that informal decision making bodies functioning on customary laws, such as khap panchayats, are refrained from enforcing their dictates, and intrusive with the right of individuals to choose their spouse.

Noting that the *Universal Declaration of Human Rights, (UDHR 1948)* affirms the principle of the inadmissibility of discrimination and inequity and proclaims that all individuals are born free and equal in dignity and rights and freedom set fourth therein, devoid of distinction of any kind including distinction based on sex. Recalling that prejudice and discrimination against women violates the principle of equality of rights and respect of human dignity, is an obstacle to the participation of women in the political, social economic and cultural life and hampers the growth and prosperity of society and the family. All crimes of honour, including honour killing, are gross violations of the rights enumerated in the declaration.

Article 1 and 2 of the declaration state that "all human beings are born free and equal in dignity and rights," and that "everyone is entitled to all the rights and freedoms set forth in" the declaration irrespective of "sex". Therefore as enumerated in the declaration's Articles 3 and 5, women are entitled to enjoy the "right to life, liberty and security of person" and also the "right to be free from torture or cruel, inhuman and or degrading treatment". Crimes of honour violate Article 3 and 5 when the purpose of the perpetrator is to inflict severe mental and physical pain on the women.

Under Article 12 of the International Convention on Economic, Social and Cultural Rights (ICESCR 1976) State parties have to take all steps to ensure the "right of everyone to the enjoyment of the highest attainable standard of physical and mental health", is ensured. Crimes of honour that involve sexual violence and mental violence or physical or mental torture obstruct the right of women to enjoy the highest attainable standard of health. India, as a State party, is therefore legally obligated to ensure that individuals and victims of crimes of honour are able to avail this right.

While not legally binding on the State, the human rights standards enumerated in paragraph 232 of the *Beijing Platform for Action (BPFA 1995)* recognises that the "human rights of women include their right to have control over and decide freely and responsibly on matters relating to their sexuality, including sexual and reproductive health, free of coercion, discrimination and violence". The Beijing Platform for Action on Women's Human Rights calls upon States to "take urgent action to combat and eliminate violence against women, which is a human rights violation resulting from harmful traditional or customary practices, cultural prejudices and extremism".

Crimes of honour may involve the violation or abuse of a number of human rights, which include the right to life, liberty and security of the person; the prohibition on torture or other cruel, inhuman, or humiliating treatment or punishment; the ban on slavery; the right to freedom from gender-based discrimination; the right to privacy; the right to marry; the right to be free from sexual abuse and exploitation; the obligation to amend customs that discriminate against women; and the right to an effective remedy. All these mentioned above violate the Human Rights Act (1998). Honour Killings are a clear violation of human rights and States necessarily need to protect individuals from such violations. Two major UN documents call for the "elimination" of honour killing. The concept of elimination appears in the *"Declaration on the Elimination of Violence against Women" (1993)* and in *"Working towards the Elimination of Crimes against Women Committed in the Name of Honour" (2003)*.

Human Rights Issues on Honour Killings

Killing in the name of honour amounts to utter rejection of "egalitarianism" - a corner stone of India's Constitution and testifies how the values of „feudalism" and "patriarchy" are rooted in our social systems and structures. Honour killings are rooted in anachronistic, antiquated attitudes and false promises. *Articles 3 and 16 of Universal Declaration of Human Rights 1948* suggest that "Everyone has the right to life, liberty and security.[cxxi] Men and women of full age without any limitation due to race, nationality or religion should have a choice to marry or to have family. They are entitled to equal rights as to marriage and dissolution. Marriage shall be entered into only with the free and full consent of the attending spouses. The family is the natural and fundamental group, unit of society and is entitled to protection by society and State.[cxxii] In the same vein, right to love and live with a person of one's choice is enshrined as a fundamental right in the Constitution. Honour killings, thus, constitute gravest disregard of universal human rights and massive violation of fundamental rights guaranteed in the Constitution. A report United Nations Population Fund (2000) estimated as many as five thousand women and girls being killed each year by relatives for dishonouring their family. Many of the cases involve the "dishonor" of having been raped.

The above examples are only a few highlighting the crimes of honour that take place in North India. If a lower-caste man is involved with a higher caste woman, he is invariably killed. And the girl, whether belonging to the higher caste or the lower caste, is also certainly eliminated.[cxxiii]

A woman's right to choose, if, when and whom to marry, is a fundamental human right. Provisions of the Indian Constitution on non-discrimination on the basis of sex, equal protection of the law, equality before the law, and the protection of life and personal liberty safeguard this right. Not only are these rights available in the constitution, but they hold a universal characteristic. Right to marry with his/her own choice was recognized in Article 1651 of the Universal Declaration of Human Rights, 1948. Article 23 of the United Nations International Covenant on Civil and Political Rights 1976 also recognizes the right of men and women of marriageable age to marry and have a family.

Contributory Factors on Honour Killing

A woman can cause that stain on the family due to several reasons, including (a) refusing to enter an arranged marriage or choosing to marry by own choice (b) engaging in certain sexual acts; (c) marrying within same "gotra" (d) seeking divorce from an abusive husband etc. Sometimes women in the family do support the honour killing of one of their own, when they agree that family is the -property and asset of only male members. Even the mother of the victim (women) may support an honour killing. In order to preserve the Honour of other female family members since many men in these societies will refuse to marry the sister of a "shamed" female whom the family has not chosen to punish, thereby "purifying" the family name by murdering the suspected female.[cxxiv]

Three main factors contribute against women in the name of honour, women's co-modification and conceptions of honour. Women are considered as the 'property of the males in their family, irrespective of their class, ethnic or religious groups. The owner of the property has the right to decide its fate. Such conceptions of women deeply inform many societies and cultures even in today's era, for example, honour killings, in countries like Syria and Pakistan are very much prevalent.

Secondly, the perception of what defines honour appears to be deeply immersed in patriarchic values and have been so widely interpreted to include male control which extends not only to the body of a woman, but all her behavior including her movements, language and actions. In any of these areas, defiance by women translates into undermining male honour and ultimately damaging the family and community honour.

Thirdly the sociologists are opined that the reason for increasing in honour killing is the fear of losing their caste status through which they gain many benefits which makes them commit this heinous crime. The other reason is because the mentality of people has not changed and they just cannot accept that marriages can take place' in the same" gotra" or outside one's caste. The root of the cause for the increase in the number of honour killings is because formal governance has not been able to reach the rural areas and as a result, this practice continues though it should have been removed by now. Also the other reason is the short-coming of official judicial system.

The resource to tribal justice and the implicit acknowledgement that rural populations fare best under this system, is widely and increasingly seen to be inefficient, expensive and inaccessible to the general public. Further one of the reasons is the increasing amongst women awareness. More women are now aware of their rights. This credit largely goes not only to the awareness raising work by women's rights groups but also to the media and mobility of women. Women's refusal to comply with the decision or traditions to violate their newly discovered rights has led to backlash from men apprehending loss of control, involving violence, killings and other such treats.

Khap Panchayats

Most of the honour killings are decided and ordered by the so-called "caste Panchayats" or "Khap Panchayats" or "Katta Panchayats" comprising members of a particular caste. Very often, these Panchayats encourage honour killings or other atrocities in an institutionalized way on boys and girls of different castes and religion, who wish to get married or have been married or interfere with the personal lives of people. These Panchayats are organized through clans and "gotras" by which they uphold social norms in the community. Such assemblies gathered on caste lines assume to themselves the power and authority to declare on and deal with objectionable matrimonies and exhibit least regard for life and liberty and are not deferred by the processes of administration of justice.

The Pernicious practice of Khap Panchayat and the like taking law into their own hands and pronouncing on the invalidity and impropriety of "Sagotra" and inter-caste marriages and handing over punishment to the couple and pressurizing the family members to execute their verdict by any means amounts to flagrant violation of rule of law and invasion of personal liberty of the persons affected. There are reports that drastic action including wrongful confinement, persistent harassment, mental torture, infliction of severe bodily harm, even like death is resorted to either by close relations or some third parties against the so-called erring couple. Social boycotts and other illegal sanctions affecting the young couple, the families and even a section, of local inhabitants are quite often faced with such depicted practices of Khap Panchayats. Khap elements zealously guard age old marital restrictions. They are fostered a culture of intolerance, making a family pariah in village' society, if its member happens to violate Khap marital norms. The family is subjected to repeated taunts, making its existence unbearable. This drives some of its members to commit murder to restore family honour. It is this social milieu spawned by Khap elements which leads to honour crimes.[cxxv]

Failure of Enforcement Agencies

A question that is asked is if a communal law which can transgress individual civil liberties is necessary when law enforcement itself is so poor.[cxxvi]

One of the major hurdles has been the way regarding the enforcement part, in which the public officials are reluctant to take on the system, accepting it as a custom - a way of life in the region, law makers and enforcement officers condone the criminality of such actions, ignoring the violent. woman-hating nature of the Khap's dictum. Criminal intimidation is a punishable offence under the Penal Code and those who provide it support can be booked for criminal conspiracy. To utter surprise, a former Police Chief of Haryana State, himself a self-styled caste leader. went on record threatening Khap-Crities. How can a former DGP publicly threaten law- abiding citizens, and yet continue to enjoy the hefty perks and pension out of the public exchequer?[cxxvii] In fact, the worst betrayal is political because caste solidarity feeds into their vote banks, and real Panchayati Raj institutions remain weak, because a Khap Panchayat is usually a collective of at least[cxxviii] or more village Panchayat. The Centre's Ministry of Home Affairs asked the Haryana Government to send its views on the issue as the centre was contemplating suggesting strict legal measures to curb the menace of honour killings perpetrated in connivance with Khap Panchayats by amending the Indian Penal Code. The Haryana Government opposed the prosecution on Khap Panchayats arguing that such a 'rash step' would disturb law and order.[cxxix]

Law Commission Recommendations

Terming the practice of khap panchayats of handing down punishment to couples who go for "sagotra" or inter-caste marriage as "flagrant violation" of the law, the Law Commission came up with a draft legislation.

The draft Prohibition of *Unlawful Assembly (interference with the freedom of matrimonial alliances) Bill, 2011* says that offences under the Act will be cognizable, non-bailable and non-compoundable: The Bill also proposes no person or "any group of persons shall gather with an intention to deliberate on, or condemn any marriage, not prohibited by law, on the basis that such marriage has dishonoured the caste or community tradition or brought disrepute to all or any of the persons forming part of the assembly or the family or the people of the locality concerned.[cxxx] Marriage, according to the draft law, includes a proposed or intended marriage.[cxxxi] The Collector or the District Magistrate has been entrusted with the responsibility of ensuring the safety of the persons targeted in case any illegal decision is taken by the khap panchayat and he/she shall take necessary steps to prohibit the convening of such illegal gatherings.[cxxxii]

Any violation of the Bill will attract imprisonment up to three years and a fine of lip to Rs. 30,000.00.[cxxxiii] All offences under the proposed Act will be cognizable, non-bailable and non-compoundable.[cxxxiv] The cases will be tried in Special Courts presided over by a sessions judge or additional sessions judge.[cxxxv] The Special Court can take suo motu cognizance of the cases. There has been a spurt in illegal intimidation by self-appointed bodies for bringing pressure against sagotra (same gotra) marriages and inter-caste, inter-community and inter-religious marriages between two consenting adults in the name of vindicating the honour of family, caste or community. In a number of cases, such bodies have resorted to incitement of violence and such newly married or couples desirous of getting married have been subjected to intimidation and violence which has also resulted into their being hounded out of their homes and sometimes even murdered.

"Although such intimidation or acts of violence constitute offences under the IPC, yet, it is necessary to prevent assemblies which take place to condemn such alliances," the proposed Bill says, adding it seeks to nip the evil in the bud and prevent spreading of hatred or incitement to violence' through such gatherings. Criminal intimidation will have the same meaning as is given in Section 503 of the IPC. The Bill further says that any member of an unlawful assembly who alone or in association with other such members counsels, exhorts or brings pressure upon any person or persons so as to prevent, or disapprove of the marriage which is objected to by the said members of the unlawful assembly, or creates an environment of hostility towards such couple shall be deemed to have acted in endangerment of their liberty.

It has suggested that an entire assembly can be deemed to be unlawful and guilty if it sits to deliberate on any marriage that is not prohibited by law. In other words, guilt will be communal and not just individual. Guilt will also be assumed until the individuals who participate in such assemblies are proven to be innocent - what is called the "reverse onus" cause. Similar provisions about placing the burden of proof on the accused to prove their innocence are present in the new draft as well, but the latter extends to murders as well. While the Law Commission acknowledges that shifting the burden of providing his/her innocence to the accused in the case of murders or in their abetment would be against the cardinal principle of jurisprudence, it argues that a presumption of guilt in participation in unlawful assemblies is necessary because obtaining eyewitnesses for the presence of individuals in those assemblies is difficult. But why cannot such an assumption hold true in the case of an honour killing itself, difficult as it is to establish guilt because of the social sway that caste/clan panchayats hold over those involved in such crimes?

Judicial Decisions

The judiciary does have a crucial role to ·play but has its limitations too. On June 23, 2006 Justice K.S. Ahluwalia of the Punjab and Haryana High Court made a revealing observation while simultaneously hearing 10 cases pertaining to marriages between young couples aged 18-21. "The High Court is flooded with petitions where ... judges of this Court have to answer for the right of life and liberty to married couples. The State is a mute spectator. When shall the State awake from its slumber [and] for how long can Courts provide solace and balm by disposing of such cases".

A recent landmark judgment by the Additional Sessions Court at Karnal in the Manoj-Babli "honour" killing case[cxxxvi], in which five accused were given the death sentence, sent shock waves among caste panhayat leaders, as it reminded them that they were not above the Constitution. The court' took serious note of the fact that the policemen deployed for the security of Manoj and Babli actually facilitated the accused in perpetrating the crime. After the judgment in the Manoj-Babli case, however a congregation of caste panchayats representing the Jat neighbourhoods from Haryana, Uttar Pradesh and Rajasthan was called at Kurukshetra on April 13. It was decided that panchayats would now fight for legal status to. legitimately maintain the "social order". One of the main agendas of this sarv-khap panchayat was to push for amendments to the Hindu Marriage Act, 1955 that would ban marriages within the same gotra (clan within which men and women are considered siblings and hence cannot marry). Under this Act, marriages between certain lineages from the paternal and maternal sides are already barred.[cxxxvii]

In *Lata Singh v. State of UP*[cxxxviii] the Supreme Court while 'speaking through Justice Markandey Katju observed:

This case reveals a shocking state of affairs. There is no dispute that the petitioner is a major and was at all relevant times a major. Hence, she is free to marry anyone she likes or live with anyone she likes. There is no bar to an inter-caste marriage under the Hindu Marriage Act or any other law. Hence, we cannot see what offence was committed by the petition, her husband or her husband's relatives.[cxxxix]

In a very recent case - *Arumugam Servai v. State of Tamil nadu*[xl] the Supreme Court strongly deprecated the practice of Khap/Katta Panchayats taking law into their own hands and indulging in offensive activities which endanger the personal lives of the persons marrying according to their choice. Justice Markandey Katju while delivering the judgment observed:

We have in recent years heard of "Khap Panchayats" (known as "Katta Panchayats" in Tamil Nadu) which often decree 'Or encourage honour killings or other atrocities in an institutionalized way on boys and girls of different castes and religion, who wish to get married or have been married, or interfere with the personal lives of people. We are of the opinion that this is wholly illegal and has to be ruthlessly stamped out. As already stated in Lata Singh case, there is nothing honourable in honour killing or other atrocities and, in fact, it is nothing but barbaric and shameful murder. Other atrocities in respect of personal lives of people committed by brutal, feudal minded persons deserve harsh punishment. Only in this way can we stamp out such' acts of barbarism and feudal mentality. Moreover, these acts take the law into their own hands, and amount to kangaroo courts, which are wholly illegal.[cxli] The Apex Court interpreted law on this matter of public concern, as: "*once a person becomes a major he or she can marry whosoever he/she likes. If the parents of the girl do not approve of such marriage the maximum they can do is that they can cut off social relations, but they cannot give threats or commit or instigate acts of violence and cannot harass the person.*" The Court observed that Khap Panchayats often decree or encourage honour killings or other atrocities in an institutionalized way on such boys and girls, who wish to get married or have been married, or interfere with the personal lives of people. This is wholly illegal and has to be ruthlessly stamped out.

In *State of UP vs. Krishna Master*[xlii] our Apex Court made an extraordinary move by awarding life sentence to the three accused of honour killing who murdered six persons of a family. The Bench further observed that "wiping out almost the whole family on the flimsy ground of saving the honour of the family would fall within the rarest of rare cases [principle] evolved by this court…" This was reiterated in *Bhagwan Das vs. State (Nct) of Delhi*[cxliii] where the Apex Court opined that "all persons who are planning to perpetrate 'honour' killings should know that the gallows await them."

Conclusion

It is the State's and the Society's responsibility to protect the human rights of its young citizens, to avoid honour killings, to create possibilities and opportunities for the people concerned to break free and to find protection, support and aid. Therefore, it is to be suggested that honour killing like social evil cannot be just eliminated through law alone rather almost every substitution social, economic, political and cultural will have to be sensitized against this crime; no doubt law could only be one of the important tools to fight this heinous practice. The usual remedies against to fight such social onslaught is to require immediate sensitization; police officials/ law enforcement agencies, setting up women police stations in the Khap belt, counseling women victims and civil administrations. Such a barbaric deeply entrenched social evil cannot brushed aside by way of more sensitization, rather the urgent requirement is active policing and penal sanction which can only antidote to this most dishonourable practice. For this it to be suggested:

1) It gives a wrong message that khap Panchayats have their own law and they adjudicate not according to laid down any procedure but summarily which they deem fit. They have scant regard to judicial institutions and courts. The steps shall be taken who so ever is involved in the crime and how so great he may be should immediately be brought under the law.

2) Special clause should be added to .section 300 of the Penal Code to deal with the cases like honour killing.

3) The onus should put on the accused persons (members of such groups/ organization/panchayats) thereby making them responsible to prove their innocence.

4) The Special Marriage Act, 1954 needs to be amended for the removal of 30 days waiting period for registering a marriage provided there is a mutual consent and both are above the legally permissible age.

ESSAY –VIII

CHILDREN AND HUMAN RIGHTS

Introduction

Child is said to father of the man. Full of potentiality children are the future of the society and the Nation. Children are tender and they depend on others for the protection of their interests, they need care, attention, protection and love. This makes the vulnerable and they can easily be neglected and exploited at any stage. Many children are not allowed to be born alive as the foetus is aborted illegally, many of them are killed or left abandoned soon after birth, they suffer from malnutrition, fall prey to trafficking, organ transplantation, neglect, sexual abuse and vices like bonded labour. The case of violation of children's rights is more sensitive because they even cannot object or report these violations. Children have all the human rights and deserve special protection also.

Children's rights are the human rights of children with particular attention to the rights of special protection and care afforded to minors. The Convention on the Rights of the Child (1989) (CRC) defines a child as any human person who has not reached the age of eighteen years. Children's rights includes their right to association with both parents, human identity as well as the basic needs for physical protection, food, universal state-paid education, health care, and criminal laws appropriate for the age and development of the child, equal protection of the child's civil rights, and freedom from discrimination on the basis of the child's race, gender, sexual orientation, gender identity, national origin, religion, disability, color, ethnicity, or other characteristics. Interpretations of children's rights range from allowing children the capacity for autonomous action to the enforcement of children being physically, mentally and emotionally free from abuse, though what constitutes "abuse" is a matter of debate. Other definitions include the rights to care and nurturing.

Sir William Blackstone (1765-9) recognized three parental duties to the child: maintenance, protection, and education. In modern language, the child has a right to receive these from the parent.

The League of Nations adopted the Geneva Declaration of the Rights of the Child (1924), which enunciated the child's right to receive the requirements for normal development, the right of the hungry child to be fed, the right of the sick child to receive health care, the right of the backward child to be reclaimed, the right of orphans to shelter, and the right to protection from exploitation.

The United Nations Universal Declaration of Human Rights (1948) in Article 25(2) recognized the need of motherhood and childhood to "special protection and assistance" and the right of all children to "social protection."

The United Nations General Assembly adopted the United Nations Declaration of the Rights of the Child (1959), which enunciated ten principles for the protection of children's rights, including the universality of rights, the right to special protection, and the right to protection from discrimination, among other rights.

Children constitute over 400 million of the one billion plus population of India. It has the highest number of children in the world. More than one third of the country's population is below 18 years. Approximately 40% of the total population i.e. around 440 million is children. India shows some of the dazzling realities of children. India has the highest rate of neo-natal deaths (around 35%) in the world. It constitutes 40% of child malnutrition in developing world. It has 50% of the child mortality. It has Reducing number of girls in 0-6 age group- for every 1000 boys 927 girls. It has 46% children from ST and 38% SC out of school. It has high number of school dropout particularly among girls. It has high rate of child marriage. Its 37% of literate & 51% of illiterate girls are married below 18 years of age. Its 10% of literate and 15% of illiterate boys are married below 18. It has large number of child laborers. It has large number of sexually abused children.[cxliv] Children's rights law is defined as the point where the law intersects with a child's life. That includes juvenile delinquency, due process for children involved in the criminal justice system, appropriate representation, and effective rehabilitative services; care and protection for children in state care; ensuring education for all children regardless of their race, gender, sexual orientation, gender identity, national origin, religion, disability, color, ethnicity, or other characteristics, and; health care and advocacy.

Who is a Child?

"A child is any human being below the age of eighteen years, unless under the law applicable to the child, majority is attained earlier." There are no definitions of other terms used to describe young people such as "adolescents", "teenagers," or "youth" in international law,[4] but the children's rights movement is considered distinct from the youth rights movement.

Biologically, a child (plural: children) is a human between the stages of birth and puberty. The legal definition of child generally refers to a minor, otherwise known as a person younger than the age of majority.[cxlv]

They are abandoned. They do not get a chance to step in a school. They are left to fend for themselves on the streets. They suffer from many forms of violence. They do not have access to even primary healthcare. They are subjected to cruel and inhumane treatments every day. They are children – innocent, young and beautiful – who are deprived of their rights.

The word 'Child' has been used in various legislation as a term denoting relationship, as a term indicating capacity, and a term of special protection. The legal conception of a child has thus tended to vary depending upon the purpose. According to Article 1 of the United Nations

Convention on the Rights of the Child 1989, 'a child means every human being below the age of eighteen years unless, under the law applicable to the child, majority is attained earlier'.

Childhood is universal transcend all nationalities and know no artificial boundaries. It is indeed an important factor in shaping the future of the nation if childhood can be endowed with the minimum requisite for healthy growth and development. Recognition of the inherent dignity and of the equal and inalienable rights of all members of the human family is the foundation of freedom, justice and peace in the world. These inalienable rights are guaranteed to all human beings including children. Children should be afforded the necessary protection and assistance for the harmonious development of their personality. [cxlvi]

Several provisions in the Constitution of India impose on the State the primary responsibility of ensuring that all the needs of children are met and that their basic human rights are fully protected. Article 21 A of the Constitution of India says that the State shall provide free and compulsory education to all children within the ages of 6 and 14 in such manner as the State may by law determine. Article 45 of the Constitution specifies that the State shall endeavour to provide early childhood care and education for all children until they complete the age of 6. Article 51 (k) lays down a duty that parents or guardians provide opportunities for education to their child/ward between the age of 6 and 14 years.

The age at which a person ceases to be a child varies under different laws in India. Under the Child Labour Prohibition and Regulation Act, 1986, a child is a person who has not completed 14 years of age. The Constitution of India protects children below the age of 14 from working in factories and hazardous jobs. But below 14, they can work in non-hazardous industries. An area of concern is that no minimum age for child labour has been specified. But for the purposes of criminal responsibility, the age limit is 7 and 12 under the Indian Penal Code, 1860. For purposes of protection against kidnapping, abduction and related offences, it's 16 years for boys and 18 for girls. For special treatment under the Juvenile Justice (Care and Protection of Children) Act 2000, the age is 18 for both boys and girls. And the Protection of Women from Domestic Violence Act 2005 defines a child as any person below the age of 18, and includes an adopted step- or foster child.

Under the Age of Majority Act 1875, every person domiciled in India shall attain the age of majority on completion of 18 years and not before. The Indian Majority Act was enacted in order to bring uniformity in the applicability of laws to persons of different religions. Unless a particular personal law specifies otherwise, every person domiciled in India is deemed to have attained majority upon completion of 18 years of age. However, in the case of a minor for whose person or property, or both, a guardian has been appointed or declared by any court of justice before the age of 18 years, and in case of every minor the superintendence of whose property has been assumed by the Court of Wards, age of majority will be 21 years and not 18.

The Hindu Minority and Guardianship Act (HMGA), 1956, in Section 4 (a), defines a 'minor' as a person who has not completed the age of 18 years.

The age of majority for the purposes of appointment of guardians of person and property of minors, according to the Dissolution of Muslim Marriages Act, 1939, is also completion of 18 years.

Christians and Parsis also reach majority at 18. Significantly, under the Child Marriage Restraint Act, 1929, which is a secular law, the age of marriage is 21 years for males and 18 years for females. But the age of marriage in Muslim personal law is the age of puberty (around 14 years). It was held that Muslims are not exempted from this law. If the marriage of a Muslim girl is performed while she is a minor, the marriage cannot be void, but the persons who participated in the marriage are not immune from the legal punishment provided under Sections 4, 5 and 6 of the Child Marriage Restraint Act. A Muslim girl can marry on attaining the age of puberty, and her marriage cannot be declared void because she is below the age of 18, according to the Child Marriage Restraint Act.

International Legal Framework and Rights of the Child

The United Nations Convention on the Rights of the Child (UNCRC) defines **Child Rights** as the minimum entitlements and freedoms that should be afforded to every citizen below the age of 18 regardless of race, national origin, colour, gender, language, religion, opinions, origin, wealth, birth status, disability, or other characteristics.

These rights encompass freedom of children and their civil rights, family environment, necessary healthcare and welfare, education, leisure and cultural activities and special protection measures. The UNCRC outlines the fundamental human rights that should be afforded to children in four broad classifications that suitably cover all civil, political, social, economic and cultural rights of every child.

International legal framework gives guidance to the local legislations. The Nations signatory to the conventions are supposed to reflect the policy of the conventions in their legislations.

The 'Declaration of the Rights of the Child, 1924', adopted by the fifth Assembly of the League of Nation, can be seen as the first International Instrument dealing with children's rights. The Declaration establishes the claim that 'mankind owes to the child the best it has to give'. This Declaration basically highlights the social and economic entitlements of children and establishes internationally the concept of the right of the child, and lays the foundation for setting the future international standards in the field of children's rights.

Another International instrument is 'Declaration of the Rights of the Child, 1959'. Its preamble describes the principle as enunciating rights and freedom, which governments should observe by legislative and other measures progressively taken. Its preamble also makes reference to both the United Nation Charter and the Universal Declaration of Human Rights. This further reiterates the pledge that, 'mankind owes to the child the best it has to give'. In accordance with the Declaration, a child is entitled to a name and nationality , to adequate nutrition, housing, recreation, and medical services , special needs of physically, mentally and 'socially handicapped' children , children who are without family etc. A noticeable departure from the principles of the 1924 Declaration is that the earlier Declaration Specified that 'Children must be the first to receive relief, whereas the 1959 Declaration lays down that children shall be 'among the first' to receive protection and relief is a good realistic approach undertaken.

In 1978, on the eve of the United Nations-sponsored International Year of the Child, a draft text was proposed for the Convention on the Rights of the Child. Drawing heavily from the Universal Declaration of Human Rights; the International Covenant on Civil and Political Rights; and the International Covenant on Economic, Social and Cultural Rights, a working group within the United Nations then collaborated and revised the draft, finally agreeing what became the articles of the Convention on the Rights of the Child. The 'Convention on the Rights of the Child, 1989', brings together the children's human rights articulated in other international instruments.

Convention on Rights of the Child

The United Nations Convention on the Rights of the Child (commonly abbreviated as the CRC, CROC, or UNCRC) is a human rights treaty which sets out the civil, political, economic, social, health and cultural rights of children. The Convention defines a child as any human being under the age of eighteen, unless the age of majority is attained earlier under a state's own domestic legislation.

Nations that ratify this convention are bound to it by international law. Compliance is monitored by the UN Committee on the Rights of the Child, which is composed of members from countries around the world. Once a year, the Committee submits a report to the Third Committee of the United Nations General Assembly, which also hears a statement from the CRC Chair, and the Assembly adopts a Resolution on the Rights of the Child. Governments of countries that have ratified the Convention are required to report to, and appear before, the United Nations Committee on the Rights of the Child periodically to be examined on their progress with regards to the advancement of the implementation of the Convention and the status of child rights in their country. Their reports and the committee's written views and concerns are available on the committee's website.

The UN General Assembly adopted the Convention and opened it for signature on 20 November 1989 (the 30th anniversary of its Declaration of the Rights of the Child). It came into force on 2 September 1990, after it was ratified by the required number of nations. Currently, 196 countries are party to it, including every member of the United Nations except the United States.

Two optional protocols were adopted on 25 May 2000. The First Optional Protocol restricts the involvement of children in military conflicts, and the Second Optional Protocol prohibits the sale of children, child prostitution and child pornography. Both protocols have been ratified by more than 150 states.

A third optional protocol relating to communication of complaints was adopted in December 2011 and opened for signature on 28 February 2012. It came into effect on 14 April 2014.

The Convention deals with the child-specific needs and rights. It requires that states act in the best interests of the child. This approach is different from the common law approach found in many countries that had previously treated children as possessions or chattels, ownership of which was sometimes argued over in family disputes.

In many jurisdictions, properly implementing the Convention requires an overhaul of child custody and guardianship laws, or, at the very least, a creative approach within the existing laws. The Convention acknowledges that every child has certain basic rights, including the right to life, his or her own name and identity, to be raised by his or her parents within a family or cultural grouping, and to have a relationship with both parents, even if they are separated.

The Convention obliges states to allow parents to exercise their parental responsibilities. The Convention also acknowledges that children have the right to express their opinions and to have those opinions heard and acted upon when appropriate, to be protected from abuse or exploitation, and to have their privacy protected, and it requires that their lives not be subject to excessive interference.

The Convention also obliges signatory states to provide separate legal representation for a child in any judicial dispute concerning their care and asks that the child's viewpoint be heard in such cases.

The Convention forbids capital punishment for children. In its General Comment 8 (2006) the Committee on the Rights of the Child stated that there was an "obligation of all state parties to move quickly to prohibit and eliminate all corporal punishment and all other cruel or degrading forms of punishment of children".Article 19 of the Convention states that state parties must "take all appropriate legislative, administrative, social and educational measures to protect the child from all forms of physical or mental violence", but it makes no explicit reference to corporal punishment.

The United Nations General Assembly in 2000 adopted two Optional Protocols to the Convention on the Child Rights to increase the protection of children from involvement in armed conflicts and from sexual exploitation.

Optional Protocol on the involvement of children in armed conflict is an effort to strengthen implementation of the Convention and increase the protection of children during armed conflicts. The Protocol requires States who ratify it to "take all feasible measures" to ensure that members of their armed forces under the age of 18 do not take a direct part in hostilities. States must also raise the minimum age for voluntary recruitment into the armed forces from 15 years but does not require a minimum age of 18.

Sale and purchase of the children is a global problem. Various international crime syndicates are involved in these crimes. Children are stolen and sold for working as forced or bonded labourers or sex workers. They are these days also trained as militants by various terrorist organizations. The 'Optional Protocol on the sale of children, child prostitution and child pornography' . The Convention's Optional Protocol on the sale of children, child prostitution and child pornography supplements the Convention by providing States with detailed requirements to end the sexual exploitation and abuse of children. It also protects children from being sold for non-sexual purposes—such as other forms of forced labour, illegal adoption and organ donation.

The Protocol defines the offences like 'sale of children', 'child prostitution' and 'child pornography'. It also creates obligations on governments to criminalize and punish the activities related to these offences. It requires punishment not only for those offering or delivering children for the purposes of sexual exploitation, transfer of organs or children for profit or forced labour, but also for anyone accepting the child for these activities.

Besides the above stated specific international instrument, some Articles of General Global Human Rights Instruments like the Universal Declaration of Human Rights, 1948; International Covenant on Economic, Social and Cultural Rights, 1966 and International Covenant on Civil and Political Rights (ICCPR), 1966 also deal with the Child Rights. Two Articles of UDHR expressly refer to children. Article 25(2) deal with special care and assistance and Article 26 on education.

Article 10 and 12 of the International Covenant on Economic, Social and Cultural Rights specifically refers to Children. Article 10 provides that states recognize the family as the 'natural and fundamental group unit of society and therefore accord the widest possible protection and assistance to the family. Article 10 (3) contains a wide ambit of protection.

Article 14 (3) (f) of ICCPR provides that criminal proceedings should take account of juveniles' age and their 'desirability of promoting their rehabilitation'. The Covenant prohibits the imposition of death penalty for crimes committed by persons below eighteen years of age. It also obliges states to separate accused juveniles from accused adults and bring them as speedily as possible for adjudication and accord them treatment according to their age and legal status .

Furthermore, one of the Regional Instrument that is 'European Convention on Human Rights', 1950 has been used as a valuable instrument for children. Part 1 enshrines the basic principle: 'Children and young person have the right to special protection against the physical and moral hazards to which they are exposed.

Classification of Rights of the Child

Child rights can be classified into four basic heads-

Right to Survival:
- Right to be born
- Right to minimum standards of food, shelter and clothing
- Right to live with dignity
- Right to health care, to safe drinking water, nutritious food, a clean and safe environment, and information to help them stay healthy

Right to Protection:
- Right to be protected from all sorts of violence
- Right to be protected from neglect
- Right to be protected from physical and sexual abuse
- Right to be protected from dangerous drugs

Right to Participation:
• Right to freedom of opinion
• Right to freedom of expression
• Right to freedom of association
• Right to information
• Right to participate in any decision making that involves him/her directly or indirectly

Right to Development:
• Right to education
• Right to learn
• Right to relax and play
• Right to all forms of development – emotional, mental and physical

Indian Scene

India ratified the Convention in 1992, agreeing in principles all articles except with certain reservations on issues relating to 'child labour'. Article 73 of the Constitution states : 'subject to the provisions of this Constitution, the executive power of the Union shall extend to the matters with respect to which Parliament has power to make laws; and to the exercise of such rights, authority and jurisdiction as are exercisable by the Government of India by virtue of any treaty or agreement'. Article 253 of the Constitution states that 'Parliament has power to make any law for the whole or any territory or any part of the territory of India for implementing any treaty, agreement to Convention with any other country or countries or any decision made at any international conference, association or other body'.

In India there is law that children under the age of 18 should not work, but there is no outright ban on child labor, and the practice is generally permitted in most industries except those deemed "hazardous".Although a law in October 2006 banned child labor in hotels, restaurants, and as domestic servants, there continues to be high demand for children as hired help in the home. Current estimates as to the number of child laborers in the country range from the government's conservative estimate of 4 million children under 14 years of age to the much higher estimates of children's rights activists, which hover around 60 million. Little is being done to address the problem since the economy is booming and the nuclear family is spreading, thereby increasing demand for child laborers. In India many people are still suffering from non-nutritious food, many parents are still leaving their children on riverside, in trains etc. Under the auspices of the Unicef financed Odisha initiative the Government of India is specifying the outline of a means of change and improvement in child care, and many trusts such as child Line, Plan India and save the children too are taking efforts to outdate child labour from India.

Article 24 of the Constitution of India makes a loud assertion for the protection of tender-aged minors and gives them a fundamental right of education and well-being. It ways - "No child below the age of fourteen years shall be allowed to work in any factory or mine or engage in any other hazardous employment".

By the 42nd Amendment Act, 1976, Article 39, in the chapter of Directive Principles of the Constitution (which contemplates common good) has been enlarged with the addition of clause (f) for the benefit of the nation's new blood in the following words:- "that children are given opportunities and facilities to develop in a healthy manner and in conditions of freedom and dignity and that childhood and youth are protected against exploitation and against moral and material abandonment".

Our constitutional courts are very conscious of the rights of children while dealing with Article 24 with Article 39(f) and 45 but there are very few enthusiasts who go for litigation in support of children. The poor parents remain silent due to their poverty, ignorance and illiteracy.

In a case decided by the Supreme Court it was held that the expression of hazardous employment is wide enough to include construction industry. The court further observed, the right of a child contained in Article 24 is endoreable even in the absence of implementing legislation and in a public interest proceeding.

Along with the Constitution of India there are various other legislations which have been enforced to protect and preserve the human rights of children. There are many important sites where the child rights violation is common in India.

Killing of the child in womb-In the Indian patriarchal families girl child is often unwelcome in many families. In spite of the Pre Natal Diagnostic Techniques Act, the people used to detect the foetus of the unborn child and if it is found to be a girl, illegal sex selective abortion is done in such cases. The government has taken many strict steps to prevent the misuse of the pre natal diagnostic techniques but still this offence has been taking place on a large scale resulting in disturbing the sex ratio also.

When the unwelcome girls are born in such cases they are treated with discrimination in comparison to their brothers. The government of India has stated various scheme to promote the bringing of children to school, the scheme like mid day meals is a successful scheme. The children of poor families are motivated by this scheme to go to school. For girl students special motivational schemes have been launced by the government ,scholarship etc is also given to them.

Right to Primary education –

The Constitution of India in a Directive Principle contained in article 45, has 'made a provision for free and compulsory education for all children up to the age of fourteen years within ten years of promulgation of the Constitution. The Government could not achieve this goal even after 50 years of adoption of this provision. Therefore the task of providing education to all children in this age group gained momentum after the National Policy of Education (NPE) was announced in 1986.
The Government of India, in partnership with the State Governments, has made strenuous efforts to fulfil this mandate and, though significant improvements were seen in various educational indicators, the ultimate goal of providing universal and quality education still remains unfulfilled.

The Constitution (Eighty-sixth Amendment) Act, 2002 inserted Article 21-A in the Constitution of India to provide free and compulsory education of all children in the age group of six to fourteen years as a Fundamental Right in such a manner as the State may, by law, determine.
With a view to making right to free and compulsory education a fundamental right, the Constitution (Eighty-third Amendment) Bill, 1997 was introduced in Parliament to insert a new article, namely, article 21 A conferring on all children in the age group of 6 to 14 years the right to free and compulsory education. The said Bill was scrutinised by the Parliamentary

Standing Committee on Human Resource Development and the subject was also dealt with in its 165th Report by the Law Commission of India.

After taking into consideration the report of the Law Commission of India and the recommendations of the Standing Committee of Parliament, the proposed amendments in
Part III, Part IV and Part IVA of the Constitution are being made which are as follows:-

(a) to provide for free and compulsory education to children in the age group of 6 to 14 years and for this purpose, a legislation would be introduced in Parliament after the Constitution (Ninety-third Amendment) Bill, 2001 is enacted;

(b) to provide in article 45 of the Constitution that the State shall endeavour to provide early childhood care and education to children below the age of six years; and

(c) to amend article 51A of the Constitution with a view to providing that it shall be the obligation of the parents to provide opportunities for education to their children.

Right to Primary education, Act-
The Constitution (Eighty-sixth Amendment) Act, 2002 inserted Article 21-A in the Constitution of India to provide free and compulsory education of all children in the age group of six to fourteen years as a Fundamental Right in such a manner as the State may, by law, determine.

Child marriages-

Poverty, weak enforcement of laws, patriarchal social norms intended to ensure family honour are significant factors that increase the risk of girl being married off while still a child. Also, girls from poor households are more likely to marry as children, since marriage becomes a solution to reduce the size of the family. The cost of marriage plays a big role in families sliding further into poverty, and these high costs contribute to girls being forced to marry when other ceremonies are taking place in the family or when older siblings are being married.[cxlvii]

The Prohibition of Child marriage Act 2006 has been made effective from 1-11-2007 in India. The object of the Act is to prohibit solemnization of child marriage and connected and incidental matters. To ensure that child marriage is eradicated from within the society, the Government of India enacted Prevention of Child marriage Act 2006 by replacing the earlier legislation of Child Marriage Restraint Act 1929.[2] This new Act is armed with enabling provisions to prohibit for child marriage, protect and provide relief to victim and enhance punishment for those who abet, promote or solemnize such marriage. This Act also calls appointment of Child Marriage Prohibition Officer for implementing this Act.

Corporeal Punishment-

Law , government and Non governmental organizations are also trying to reduce the child marriages. Along with these violations children are also being subjected to corporeal punishments, which has been discouraged in the schools and at home now. In the case *Parent forum vs. Union of India*[cxlviii] the High Court of Delhi held that freedom of life and liberty guaranteed by Article 21 is not only violated when physical punishment scars the body , but that freedom is also violated when that freedom scars the mind of the child and robs him of his dignity. Any act of violence that traumatizes, terrorizes a child or adversely affects his faculties falls foul of article 21.

Child Labour-Because most of the Indian housed are still below the poverty line , children are compelled to work in order to continue in the family income. Making right to education compulsory has reduced child labour. Various other laws are also trying to stop child labour.

Section 67 of the Factories Act, 1948 explicitly prohibited the employment of children below the age of 14 years in factories. But this law was not followed in the match, bangles and electric bulbs manufacturing establishments. It took our central legislators over two decades to enact the Child Labour (Prohibition and Regulation) Act, 1986.

Many children in India work as child labours. At Railway stations at bus terminals children below the age of 14 years are engaged in roadside eating houses and tea-stalls. Children are employed in match and fireworks, carpet weaving, beedi rolling, diamomd industry (Gujarat) and in various other parts of the country in silver chain industry, textiles, powerlooms, handlooms, lorry body- building workshops, garages, domestic work, brick kilns and dyeing units.

In *People's Union for Democratic Rights and others Vs. Union of India and others* [cxlix] otherwise referred to as the Asiad Workers Case, the Supreme Court said, "We are, therefore, of the view that when a person provides labour of service to another for remuneration which is lees than the minimum wage, the labour or service provided by him clearly falls within the scope and ambit of the words "forced labour" under Article 23 (of the Constitution of India)."

In *Bandhua Mukti Morcha Vs. Union of India and others* [cl], the Supreme Court held "Therefore, whenever it is shown that the labourer is made to provide forced labour, the Court would raise a presumption that he is required to do so in consideration of an advance or other economic consideration received by him and he is, therefore, a bonded labour. This presumption may be rebutted by the employer and also by the State Government if it so chooses but unless and until satisfactory material is provided for rebutting this presumption, the Court must proceed on the basis that the labourer is a bonded labourer entitled to the benefit of provisions of the Act. The State Government cannot be permitted to repudiate its obligation to identify, release and rehabilitate the bonded labourers on the plea that though the concerned labourers may be providing forced labour, the State Government does not owe any obligation to them unless and until they show in an appropriate legal proceeding conducted according to the rules of adversary system of justice, that they are bonded labourers."

The above two judgments of the Supreme Court of India lay down the law, in terms of Article 141 of the Constitution of India, to the effect that:-

(a) Where a person gets a remuneration which is less than the current notified minimum wage under the Minimum Wages Act, 1984 for the particular scheduled employment, the labour or service provided by that person clearly falls within the ambit of the term 'forced labour under Article 23 of the Constitution, and

(b) Where a labourer is made to provide forced labour, he is presumed to be a bonded labourer in terms of the Bonded Labour System (Abolition) Act. 1976.

In *M.C. Mehta V/s the State of Tamil Nadu and others* a three Judge Bench of the Supreme Court, consisting of Justices Kuldip Singh, B.L. Hansaria and S.B. Majumdar, handed over to the nation a landmark judgement the essence of which is that children below 14 years cannot be employed in any factory or mine or hazardous work and that they must be given education as mandated by Article 45.

For the children employed in non-hazardous jobs, the Court further directed that the Inspector (as provided in the Child Labour Prohibition and Regulation Act, 1986) shall have to see that the working hours of the child are not more than four to six hours a day and he or she receives education at least for two hours each day, the entire cost of which will be borne by the employer.

In *Court on its own motion v Govt. of NCT Delhi*, Writ Petition[cli]Apex court commented that ,today's children constitute tomorrow's future. To ensure a bright future of our children, we have to ensure that they are educated and not exploited. It was also held that , children are the most vulnerable members of any society.

They are entitled to special care and assistance because of their physical and mental immaturity. The problem is more complicated in developing countries like ours, where child labour exists in
relationship with illiteracy and poverty. The court gave the directive to eliminate the menace of child labour and to effectuate the mandate of Articles 23, 24, 39, 45 and 47 of the Constitution.

Supreme Court had given a large number of mandatory directions in *M.C. Mehta v. State of Tamil Nadu* [clii]. One of the important directions was to direct an employer to pay a compensation of Rs. 20,000/- for having employed a child below the age of 14 years hazardous work in contravention of Child Labour (Prohibition & Regulation) Act, 1986 .

The appropriate Government was also directed to contribute a grant/deposit of Rs. 5,000/-for each such child employed in a hazardous job. The said sum of Rs. 25,000/- was to be deposited in a fund to be known as Child Labour Rehabilitation-cum-Welfare Fund and the income from such corpus was to be used for rehabilitation of the rescued child.

In a UN publication (August, 1998) titled 'Position Paper On Child Labour In India', the following approaches were suggested for the uplift of the neglected youths: Promotion and enhancement of education, strengthening of national and international legislation and improved enforcement, empowerment of the poor, social mobilization and community sensitization against all forms of child labour, advocacy for increased responsibility among employers and corporations, and general advocacy and awareness generation.

Discrimination-

In the case, *Gaurav Jain and Supreme Court Bar Association versus Union of India and Ors.* [cliii] the SC stated in its order dated 15-11-1989 that "segregating children of prostitutes by locating separate schools and providing separate hostels would not be in the interest of the children and the society at large". While the SC did not accept the plea for separate hostels for children of prostitutes, it felt that "accommodation in hostels and other reformatory homes should be adequately available to help segregation of these children from their mothers living in prostitute homes as soon as they are identified. The court held that women found in the flesh trade, should be viewed more as victims of adverse socio-economic circumstances rather than as offenders in our society. Equally, the right of the child is the concern of the society so that fallen women surpass trafficking of her person from exploitation; contribute to bring up her children; live a life with dignity; and not to continue in the foul social environment. Equally, the children have the right to equality of opportunity, dignity and care, protection and rehabilitation by the society with both hands open to bring them into the mainstream of social life without pre-stigma affixed on them for no fault of her/his.

Juvenile Delinquency-

Juvenile Justice (Care and Protection of Children) Act, 2015 is a proposed Act of the Parliament of India. It aims to replace existing the Indian juvenile delinquency law, Juvenile Justice (Care and Protection of Children) Act, 2000, so that juveniles in conflict with Law in the age group of 16–18, involved in Heinous Offences, can be tried as adults. The Act came into force from 15 January 2016.

It was passed on 7 May 2015 by the Lok Sabha amid intense protest by several Members of Parliament. It was passed on 22 December 2015 by the Rajya Sabha.

After the 2012 Delhi gang rape, it was found that one of the accused was a few months away from being 18. So, he was tried in a juvenile court.

The bill will allow a Juvenile Justice Board, which would include psychologists and sociologists, to decide whether a juvenile criminal in the age group of 16–18 should tried as an adult or not. The bill introduced concepts from theHague Convention on Protection of Children and Cooperation in Respect of Inter-Country Adoption, 1993 which were missing in the previous act. The bill also seeks to make the adoption process of orphaned, abandoned and surrendered children more streamlined.

Child Sexual Abuse-

Child sexual abuse laws in India have been enacted as part of the nation's child protection policies. The Parliament of India passed the 'Protection of Children Against Sexual Offences Bill, 2011' regarding child sexual abuse on May 22, 2012 into Act. The rules formulated by the government in accordance with the law have also been notified on 14th November 2012 and the law has become ready for implementation. Fifty three percent of children in India face some form of child sexual abuse.The need for stringent law has been felt many times.

Child sexual abuse was prosecuted under the following sections of Indian Penal Code:

- I.P.C. (1860) 375- Rape
- I.P.C. (1860) 354- Outraging the modesty of a woman
- I.P.C. (1860) 377- Unnatural offences
- I.P.C. (1860) 511- Attempt

The new Act provides for a variety of offenses under which an accused can be punished. It recognizes forms of penetration other than peno-vaginal penetration and criminalizes acts of immodesty against children too. The legislators tried to draft a gender-neutral Act, but failed, using the pronoun 'he' in the description of various offenses. With respect to pornography, the Act criminalizes even watching or collection of pornographic content involving children.The Act makes abettment of child sexual abuse an offense . It also provides for various procedural reforms,making the tiring process of trial in India considerably easier for children. The Act has been criticized as its provisions seem to criminalize consensual sexual intercourse between two people below the age of 18. The 2001 version of the Bill did not punish consensual sexual activity if one or both partners were above 16 years.

The newly passed Information Technology Bill is set to make it illegal to not only create and transmit child pornography in any electronic form, but even to browse it. The punishment for a first offence of publishing, creating, exchanging, downloading or browsing any electronic depiction of children in "obscene or indecent or sexually explicit manner" can attract five years in jail and a fine of Rs 10 lakh.

National Commission for Protection of Child Rights (NCPCR)

NCPCR is an Indian governmental commission, established by an Act of Parliament, the Commission for Protection of Child Rights Act in December 2005. The Commission began operation a year later in March 2007. The Commission considers that its Mandate is "to ensure that all Laws, Policies, Programmes, and Administrative Mechanisms are in consonance with the Child Rights perspective as enshrined in the Constitution of India and the UN Convention on the Rights of the Child.

Conclusion

There is a need to make people aware about the child rights and the schemes made by the government for the children must be publicized well. Most of the people are not aware of the schemes so they are not able to take any benefit of them. Presently we have proper legislative framework to protect the children. The enforcement mechanism must be made strong and more effective.

Children with disabilities (blind, handicapped or mentally retarded children) are the worst affected segments amongst the whole population of children. They should be given special protection and attention so that they can be effectively trained to develop their capacities and earn their livelihood in future, this will prevent them from becoming burden on the society when they grow up. Many NGO's and INGO's have programmes to support the needy children. Poverty, ignorance and insincere leadership stand as great challenges. Parents should also know the importance of proper childcare. Media can also play great responsibility in educating the people about child rights. More programmes should be broadcasted and telecasted to make children vigilant about their rights in a non formal way. Children should be taught to defend themselves intelligently so that they should not fall prey to the antisocial elements of the society.

Essay –IX

RIGHT TO CLEAN ENVIRONMENT

Man's paradise is on earth; This living world is the beloved place of all; It has the blessings of Nature's bounties: Live in a lovely spirit.[cliv]

Link Between Environmental Protection and Human rights [clv]
International environmental law and human rights law have intertwined objectives and
ultimately strive to produce better conditions of life on earth. They both seek to tackle
universal challenges that must often be solved at the same time at the individual and
global level. The necessity to link both fields stems from the different, complementary
and partial approaches each has attempted to follow. Environmental law seeks to protect
both nature for itself, and for the benefit of humankind on a local and global scale. It has
broadly been confined to regulating inter-state relations and, of late, the behaviour of
some economic actors.
Human rights have centred on fundamental aspirations of human beings with much more developed compliance mechanisms allowing individuals and groups to claim their rights. The inclusion of an environmental dimension in the human rights debate has become necessary in view of the recognition of the pervasive influence of local and global environmental conditions upon the realization of human rights. In legal

terms, the new linkages will come to enhance the protection in both fields as the protection of the environment will benefit from the established machinery whereas the human rights system will be enhanced by the inclusion of new interpretative elements until recently ignored.
Different avenues for the integration of environmental concerns in the realization of
human rights can be envisaged. Firstly, a reinterpretation of human rights included in
international instruments can be attempted. Environmental conservation is hereby included
as a further interpretative element widening the scope of the rights. Second, some
procedural rights developed separately in human rights and environmental law instruments
could be used in conjunction to form a body of very effective technical rights. Finally,
a right to environment may be formally added to the catalogue of internationally
guaranteed human rights. While each approach can be to some extent pursued separately,
they all tend towards the same goal.[clvi]

Foundation of the Claim

On a factual level, it has already become apparent that preservation, conservation and
restoration of the environment are a necessary and integral part of the enjoyment of, *inter
alia*, the rights to health, to food and to life including a decent quality of life.' The close
link with these rights clearly shows that a right to environment can easily be incorporated
into the core of the human rights protection whose ultimate purpose is the blooming of
the personality of all human beings in dignity.'
In accordance with international law theory, all human rights represent universal
claims necessary to grant every human being a decent life that are part of the core moral
codes common to all societies.' International human rights have been based, since their
inception, on this premise that should not be seen as another manifestation of
imperialism,' but as the recognition that all human beings aspire to a life in dignity.'

The linkage between environmental and human rights concerns has so far been envisaged
mostly in terms of the protection or conservation of a clean or healthy environment for
the benefit of individuals whose conditions of life are threatened, *e.g.* by noise
disturbances or air pollution arising from airports or motorways and industrial pollution.
To arrive at a truly universal formulation, a right to environment should also encompass
other issues of concern to a majority of the world's population, including access to fresh
water and food supplies.
The apparently sharp difference between industry-related pollution seen mainly as a
problem of the North and livelihoods issues perceived as a southern issue prompts some
to claim that problems are too divergent in North and South countries to be dealt within
a single framework. This criticism overlooks the fact that many environmental problems
are not country-specific and that industrial pollution is in most cases experienced in a
similar fashion throughout the world even if southern countries may be less preoccupied
with industrial pollution **than** with other more pressing issues.[clvii]

International Legal fFamework

Fifty years ago, the concept of a human right to a healthy environment was viewed as a novel, even radical, idea. Today it is widely recognized in international law and endorsed by an overwhelming proportion of countries. Even more importantly, despite their recent vintage, environmental rights are included in more than 90 national constitutions. These provisions are having a remarkable impact, ranging from stronger environmental laws and landmark court decisions to the cleanup of pollution hot spots and the provision of safe drinking water.[1]

Environmental rights and responsibilities have been a cornerstone of indigenous legal systems for millennia.[2] Yet the right to a healthy environment is not found in pioneering human rights documents such as the *Universal Declaration of Human Rights* (1948), the *International Covenant on Civil and Political Rights* (1966), or the *International Covenant on Economic, Social, and Cultural Rights* (1966). Society's awareness of the magnitude, pace, and adverse consequences of environmental degradation was not sufficiently advanced during the era when these agreements were drafted to warrant the inclusion of ecological concerns.

The first written suggestion that there should be a human right to a healthy environment came from Rachel Carson in *Silent Spring*, published in 1962:

If the Bill of Rights contains no guarantees that a citizen shall be secure against lethal poisons distributed either by private individuals or by public officials, it is surely only because our forefathers, despite their considerable wisdom and foresight, could conceive of no such problem.

Similarly, in her final public speech before dying of cancer, Carson testified before President Kennedy's Scientific Advisory Committee, urging it to consider

a much neglected problem, that of the right of the citizen to be secure in his own home against the intrusion of poisons applied by other persons. I speak not as a lawyer but as a biologist and as a human being, but I strongly feel that this is or ought to be one of the basic human rights.

The first formal recognition of the right to a healthy environment came in the *Stockholm Declaration*, which emerged from the pioneering global eco-summit in 1972:

Man has the fundamental right to freedom, equality and adequate conditions of life, in an environment of a quality that permits a life of dignity and well-being, and he bears a solemn responsibility to protect and improve the environment for present and future generations.5

In the four decades since the *Stockholm Declaration*, the right to a healthy environment rapidly migrated around the globe. As of 2012, 177 of the world's 193 UN member nations recognize this right through their constitution, environmental legislation, court decisions, or ratification of an international agreement.[6]

Regional human rights agreements recognizing the right to a healthy environment have been ratified by more than 130 nations spanning Europe, Asia, the Americas, the Caribbean, Africa, and the Middle East. The Inter-American Commission on Human Rights, the Inter-American Court of Human Rights, the African Commission on Human and Peoples Rights, the European Court of Human Rights, and the European Committee on Social Rights have issued decisions in cases involving violations of this right.

The resolution 16/11 adopted by the Human Rights Council on 12th of April 2011 entitled "Human Rights and the environment" requested the Office of the High Commissioner "in consultation with and taking into account the views of States Members of the United Nations, relevant international organizations and intergovernmental bodies, including the

United Nations Environment Programme and relevant multilateral environmental agreements, special procedures, treaty bodies and other stakeholders, to conduct, within existing resources, a detailed analytical study on the relationship between human rights and the environment" (para.1).

The Office of the United Nations High Commissioner for Human Rights would be grateful to receive any relevant information for the preparation of this study. In particular, views and information would be welcome on:

Steps taken at national and regional levels, including in the normative, legislative and judicial spheres, to better understand and address the relationship between human rights and the environment;

Views on the relationship between human rights obligations and environmental protection, including issues related to international cooperation of States in respect to global environmental harms (such as climate change-related harms) and other key areas of environmental policy such as biodiversity, ecosystem services and desertification;

Choices made by governments and other actors that effect the environment, or that frame responses to environmental challenges, impact directly on the realization of human rights. The link between the environment and human rights has long been recognized. The Stockholm Declaration of the United Nations Conference on the Human Environment, Stockholm (1972), and to a lesser extent the Rio Declaration on Environment and Development (1992), show how the link between human rights and dignity and the environment was very prominent in the early stages of United Nations efforts to address environmental problems.

Since 1989, the Commission on Human Rights started to address environmental issues through resolutions on movement and dumping of toxic and dangerous products and wastes (Resolution - 1989/42). The Commission on Human Rights adopted its first resolution entitled *Human rights and the environment* in 1994 followed by a number of resolutions on the same subject matter in 1995 and 1996 (Res. 1994/65; Res. 1995/14; Res. 1996/13).

From 2002, the Year of the World Summit on Sustainable Development, the Commission on Human Rights adopted resolutions on the environment that were entitled *Human rights and the environment as part of sustainable development* (Res. 2002/75; Res. 2003/71; Res. 2005/60).

Constitution of India and Human Right to Clean Environment

While international law plays a vital role in establishing norms and offering a court of last resort for human rights violations, the reality is that most of the action to protect and fulfill rights occurs at the national level. Within countries, a constitution is the highest and strongest law, as all laws, regulations, and policies must be consistent with it. A constitution protects human rights, sets forth the obligations of the state, and restricts government powers. On a deeper level, constitutions reflect the most deeply held and cherished values of a society. As a judge once stated, "A constitution is a mirror of a nation's soul."[7]

Portugal (in 1976) and Spain (1978) were the first countries to include the right to a healthy environment in their constitutions. Article 66 of Portugal's Constitution states, "Everyone has the right to a healthy and ecologically balanced environment and the duty to defend it."[8] Since the mid-1970s, 92 countries have granted constitutional status to this right (see Figure 2). Constitutional law experts observe that recognition of environmental rights has grown more rapidly over the past 50 years than any other human right.[9]

The Constitution of India originally adopted, did not contain any direct and specific provision regarding the protection of natural environment. Perhaps, the framers of the Indian Constitution, at that time, considered it as a negligible problem. That is probably why it did not even contain the expression environment. However, in fact it contained only a few Directives to the State on some aspects relating to public health, agriculture and animal husbandry. These Directives were and are still not judicially enforceable.

Nevertheless, on a careful analysis of various provisions prior to the 42nd Constitutional Amendment, reveals that some of the Directive Principles of State Policy showed a slight inclination towards environmental protection. It can be inferred from Art 39(b), Art 47, Art 48 and Art 49 . These directive principles individually and collectively impose a duty on the State to create conditions to improve the general health level in the country and to protect and improve the natural environment.

Regarding the expression material resources of the community present in Art 39(b) it was held in *Assam Sillimanite Ltd. v. Union of India* that material resources embraces all things, which are capable of producing wealth for the community. It has been held to include such resources in the hands of the private persons and not only those, which have already vested in the State.

The Supreme Court in Municipal Council, *Ratlam v. Vardhichand* observed that the State will realise that Art 47 makes it a paramount principle of governance that are steps taken for the improvement of public health as amongst its primary duties

From these Articles, one can understand that the Constitution of India was not as environmentally blind as suggested by some eminent jurists. Though the word environment was not expressly used in the Constitution, the object of the above Articles was to conserve the natural resources, thereby protecting the environment. However, it must be accepted that only with the strengthening of public interest litigations and an enhanced commitment from the Central Government during the late 1970s, did an expansion of constitutional provisions to include aspects relating to the environment take place.

Forty-Second Constitutional Amendment
Taking note of the Stockholm Conference and the growing awareness of the environmental crises, the Indian Constitution was amended in the year 1976. This gave it an environmental dimension and added to it direct provisions for the preservation of ecological and biological diversity.

Art 48A, a directive principle, was inserted into Part IV of the Constitution, reading as follows: The State shall endeavour to protect and improve the environment and to safeguard the forests and wildlife of the country. Correspondingly, an obligation was imposed on the State through Art 51 A(g) in Part IVA, casts a duty on every citizen of India stating: It shall be the duty of every citizen of India to protect and improve the natural environment including forests, lakes, rivers and wildlife and to have compassion for living creatures.

In *M.K. Janardhanam v. District Collector, Tiruvallur*, the Madras High Court has observed that the phrase used (in Art 48A and Art 51A) is protect and improve which implies that the phrase appears to contemplate affirmative governmental action to improve the quality of the environment and not just to preserve the environment in its degraded form. Therefore, the constitution makes two fold provisions - On one hand, it gives directive to the State for the protection and improvement of environment and on the other, it casts a duty on every citizen to help in the preservation of natural environment.

Environment Policy

In the early years of Indian independence, there was no precise environmental policy. Government tried to make attempts only from time to time as per the growing needs of the society. The period of 1970s witnessed a lot of changes in policies and attitudes of the Indian Government when its attitude changed from environmental indifference to greater and subsequently, manifold steps were taken to improve environmental conditions.

National Committee on Environmental Planning and Coordination The year 1972 marks a watershed in the history of environmental management in India. This is because prior to 1972, environmental concerns such as sewage disposal, sanitation and public health were dealt with by different federal ministries and each pursued these objectives in the absence of a proper coordination system at the federal or the intergovernmental level. When the twenty-fourth UN General Assembly decided to convene a conference on the human environment in 1972, and requested a report from each member country on the state of environment, a Committee on human environment under the chairmanship of Pitambar Pant, member of the Planning Commission, was set up to prepare India's report. With the help of the reports, the impact of the population explosion on the natural environment and the existing state of environmental problems were examined.

By early 1972, it had been realised that unless a national body was established to bring about greater coherence and coordination in environmental policies & programmes and to integrate environmental concerns, an important lacuna would remain in India's planning process. Consequently, as a result of the major issues highlighted by the reports, a National Committee on Environmental Planning and Coordination (NCEPC) was established in the Department of Science and Technology.

The NCEPC is an apex advisory body in all matters relating to environmental protection and improvement. At its inception, the Committee consisted of fourteen members drawn from various disciplines concerning environmental management. Most of the non-official members were specialists. The Committee was to plan and coordinate, but the responsibility for execution remained with various ministries and government agencies.

Environmental Legislations

Derived from the Right to Life , implies the right to live without the deleterious invasion of pollution, environmental pollution, environmental degradation and ecological imbalances. Everyone has the right to life and a right standard of living adequate for health & well being of himself and of his family. States should recognise everybody's right to an adequate standard and to continuous improvement of living conditions. Thus, inherent right to life shall be protected by law.

As part of its campaign on green environment, Indian Parliament has enacted nation wide comprehensive laws. One of the major environmental enactments came just two years after the Stockholm Conference in 1974. The Water (Prevention and Control of Pollution) Act was passed for the purpose of prevention and control of water pollution and for maintaining and restoring the wholesomeness of water. The Water Act represented India's first attempt to deal with an environmental issue from a legal perspective.

From this period onwards, the Central Government has been considered as highly environmentally active. In 1976, the Constitution of India was amended to insert a separate fundamental duties chapter. The 1980s witnessed the creation of many eco-specific organizations. In the year 1980, the Forest (Conservation) Act was passed for the conservation of forests and to check on further deforestation. The Air (Prevention and Control of Pollution) Act of 1981 was enacted by invoking the Central Government's power under Art 253. The Air Act contained several distinguishing features. The preamble of the Air Act explicitly reveals that the Act represents an implementation of the decisions made at the Stockholm Conference. Also, a notification relating to Noise Pollution (Regulation & Control) Rules was made in the year 2000 with the objective of maintaining Ambient Air Quality Standards in respect of noise.

In the wake of the Bhopal gas tragedy, the Government of India enacted the Environment (Protection) Act, 1986. The laws that existed prior to the enactment of EPA essentially focused on specific pollution (such as air and water). The need for a single authority which could assume the lead role for environmental protection was answered through the enactment of EPA. It is in the form of an umbrella legislation designed to provide a framework for Central Government to coordinate the activities of various central and state authorities established under previous laws. It is also in the form of an enabling law, which delegates wide powers to the executive to enable bureaucrats to frame necessary rules and regulations.

Apart from this, several notifications and rules have also been made, some of which include the Hazardous Wastes (Management and Handling) Rules in 1989, the Biomedical Wastes (Management and Handling) Rules in 1998, Recycled Plastics (Manufacture and Usage) Rules 1999, Environment (Silting for Industrial Projects) Rules 1999 and the Municipal Solid Wastes (Management and Handling) Rules in 2000.In addition to these eco-specific legislations, realising that there is no comprehensive legislation dealing with biodiversity in India, and to fulfil its international obligation under the Convention on Bio-Diversity, the Government of India has enacted the Biological Diversity Act, 2002.

It is a paradox that despite the presence of such diverse laws, the pollution rate has crossed the dead line. This is probably because of the reason that the law is so complicated and vague that even the expert may not know the intricacies of it.

Contribution of Judiciary

The judiciary, to fulfill its constitutional obligations was and is always prepared to issue appropriate orders, directions and writs against those persons who cause environmental pollution and ecological imbalance. This is evident from a plethora of cases decided by starting from the Ratlam Municipality Case. This case provoked the consciousness of the judiciary to a problem which had not attracted much attention earlier. The Supreme Court responded with equal anxiety and raised the issue to come within the mandate of the Constitution.

Judicial activism in India provides an impetus to the campaign against pollution. The path for people's involvement in the judicial process has been shown. If this had not been done so, the system would have collapsed and crumbled under the burden of its insensitivity.

The right to live in a clean and healthy environment is not a recent invention of the higher judiciary in India. The right has been recognised by the legal system and the judiciary in particular for over a century or so. The only difference in the enjoyment of the right to live in a clean and healthy environment today is that it has attained the status of a fundamental right the violation of which, the Constitution of India will not permit.

It was only from the late eighties and thereafter, various High Courts and the Supreme Court of India have designated this right as a fundamental right. Prior to this period, as pointed out earlier, people had enjoyed this right not as a constitutionally guaranteed fundamental right but as a right recognised and enforced by the courts under different laws like Law of Torts, Indian Penal Code, Civil Procedure Code, Criminal Procedure Code etc. In today's emerging jurisprudence, environmental rights which encompass a group of collective rights are described as third generation rights.

Right to Environment - As a Fundamental Right guaranteed in Indian Constitution

Environmental values or rights may be constitutionalised either explicitly by amending the constitution or implicitly by interpreting the existing constitutional language to include environmental protection. Immediately after the Stockholm Declaration, there was a growing trend in national legal systems to give constitutional status to environmental protection. India followed in the pursuit by amending the Constitution to include environment specific provisions in 1976. The birth of right to environment was the direct result of an inclusion these additional provisions.

The Indian Supreme Court, being one of the most active judiciaries in the world, also created a landmark in the quest of international judicial activism by developing the concept of right to healthy environment as a part of right to life under Art 21 of our Constitution. Art 21 reads as follows:

No person can be deprived of his life and personal liberty except according to the procedure established by law.

Thus, in India, the higher judiciary has interpreted Art 21 to give it an expanded meaning of including the right to a clean, safe and healthy environment. Class actions have been entertained by the Supreme Court under Art 32 of the Constitution as being part of public interest litigation actions. The High Courts, also being granted this jurisdiction under Art 226 have intervened by passing writs, orders and directions in appropriate cases, thereby giving birth to an incomparable environmental jurisprudence in the form of the constitutional right to healthy environment. A chronological analysis of the environmental mission of the courts has been undertaken in order to explicate the development of the ideology of right to environment as being part of the right to life in the Indian context.

Keeping this in regard, the first case of considerable importance is *Ratlam Municipality v. Virdhichand*,[clviii] the matter came up by way of a criminal appeal, where the Supreme Court gave directions for the removal of open drains and for prevention of public excretion by the slum dwellers. In giving the judgement, the Court relied upon Art 47 in Part IV of the Constitution. The decision given by the Supreme Court in *Sachidanand Pandey v. State of West Bengal*,[clix] seemed to be narrowing the level of scrutiny as opposed to enlarging it to include the all pervasive environmental dimension. In this case, the proposal for the construction lodging by the Taj Group of Hotels, amidst the zoological gardens of Allipore, for improving tourism in West Bengal was accepted by the Government and subsequently, when the case appeared before the Supreme Court, the decision of the Tourism Ministry was upheld. The Court justified its stand that appropriate considerations had been borne in mind and irrelevancies were excluded.

However, one must not be misled in thinking that the decision of the court in Sachidanand Pandey case suppressed its activist nature. This decision is no longer an authority as the limited nature of scrutiny is not followed by the Courts of the present years. Independent specialists and expert committees are appointed in order to determine whether the claims of the aggrieved parties are actually genuine to be addressable in court.

Bhagwati,CJ in *M.C.Mehta vs. Union of India and Shriram Foods & Fertilizers*[clx] Case observed:

"We would also suggest to the Government of India that since cases involving issues of environmental pollution, ecological destructions and conflicts over national resources are increasingly coming up for adjudication and these cases involve assessment and evolution of scientific and technical data, it might be desirable to set up Environmental Courts on the regional basis with one professional Judge and two experts drawn from the Ecological Sciences Research Group keeping in view the nature of the case and the expertise required for its adjudication. There would of course be a right of appeal to this Court from the decision of the Environment Court."

In other words, this Court not only contemplated a combination of a Judge and Technical Experts but also an appeal to the Supreme Court from the Environmental Court.

M.C. Mehta v. UOI[clxi] With a view to check rapid deterioration of air quality in Delhi, which was becoming a health hazard besides being an environmental enemy certain directions have been issued by this Court from time to time in the main Writ Petition.

The Committee may submit a report to this Court in that behalf as also indicate as to which fuel can be regarded as "clean fuel", which does not cause pollution or is otherwise injurious to health. Let the report be submitted within one month.

On the basis of the report of the Bandopadhyay Committee, in *Rural Litigation Entitlement Kendra v. State of U.P.*[clxii], a case relating to the exploitation of limestone from the Dehradun area and its adverse effect on the ecology and environment, the Supreme Court stated that environment assets are permanent assets of mankind and are not intended to be exhausted in one generation....Preservation of the environment and keeping the ecological balance unaffected is a task which not only Governments but also every citizen must undertake. The Supreme Court, in this case ordered the closure of certain limestone quarries causing large scale pollution and adversely affecting the safety and health of the people living in the area. Likewise, in M.C. Mehta v. Union of India, the court directed an industry manufacturing hazardous and lethal chemicals and gases posing danger to health and life of workmen and people living in its neighbourhood, to take all necessary safety measures before reopening the plant. In an attempt to maintain the purity and holiness of the River Ganga, tanneries polluting the sacred river were ordered to be closed down.

Absolute liability for the harm caused by an industry engaged in hazardous and inherently dangerous activities became a newly formulated doctrine, free from the exceptions to the strict liability rule. As a result, the exceptions to the strict liability rule are no longer applicable in India in those cases determining the liability of hazardous and inherently dangerous industries. Thus, in a passive way, the right of citizens to live in a wholesome and healthy environment was recognized and steps were taken to protect them from the hazards of polluting industries.

For the first time in the case of *Subash Kumar v. State of Bihar*[lxiii], the court declared that the right to life under Art 21 includes the right to clean water and air. In the same case, the rule of locus standi was enlarged so that the court could take cognizance of environmental degradation and regulate the prevention of the same in an effective manner. In Virender Gaur v. State of Haryana[clxiv], the Apex Court confirmed that for every citizen, there exists a constitutional right to healthy environment and further conferred a mandatory duty on the state to protect and preserve this human right. Holding that the Government has no power to sanction lease of the land vested in the Municipality for being used as open space for public use, the Supreme Court in *Virender Gaur v. State of Haryana*, the Court explicitly held that: The word environment is of broad spectrum which brings within its ambit hygienic atmosphere and ecological balance. It is therefore, not only the duty of the State but also duty of every citizen to maintain hygienic environment. The State, in particular has duty in that behalf and to shed its extravagant unbridled sovereign power and to forge in its policy to maintain ecological balance and hygienic environment.

A foundation for the application of the Precautionary Principle, the Polluter Pays Principle and Sustainable Development, having been laid down, the three principles were applied together for the first time in by the Supreme Court in Vellore Citizens Welfare Forum v. Union of India, a case concerning pollution being cause due to the discharge of untreated effluents from tanneries in the state of Tamil Nadu. The Court, referring to the precautionary principle, polluter pays principle and the new concept of onus of proof, supported with the constitutional provisions of Art. 21, 47, 48A and 51A (g) and declared that these doctrines have become part of the environmental law of the country.

The Public Trust Doctrine, evolved in *M.C. Mehta v. Kamal Nath*, states that certain common properties such as rivers, forests, seashores and the air were held by Government in Trusteeship for the free and unimpeded use of the general public. Granting lease to a motel located at the bank of the River Beas would interfere with the natural flow of the water and that the State Government had breached the public trust doctrine.

A matter regarding the vehicular pollution in Delhi city, in the context of Art 47 and 48 of the Constitution came up for consideration in *M.C. Mehta vs. Union of India* (Vehicular Pollution Case). It was held to be the duty of the Government to see that the air did not become contaminated due to vehicular pollution. The Apex court again confirming the right to healthy environment as a basic human right, stated that the right to clean air also stemmed from Art 21 which referred to right to life. This case has served to be a major landmark because of which lead-free petrol supply was introduced in Delhi. There was a complete phasing out old commercial vehicles more than 5 years old as directed by the courts. Delhi owes its present climatic conditions to the attempt made to maintain clean air.

In the very recent case of T.N. Godavarman Thirumulpad v. Union of India, a case concerning conservation of forests, Justice Y.K. Sabharwal, held: ...Considering the compulsions of the States and the depletion of forest, legislative measures have shifted the responsibility from States to the Centre. Moreover any threat to the ecology can lead to violation of the right of enjoyment of healthy life guaranteed under Art 21, which is required to be protected. The Constitution enjoins upon this Court a duty to protect the environment.

Moreover in *S. Jagannath v. Union of India*, the Supreme Court has held that setting up of shrimp culture farms within the prohibited areas and in ecologically fragile coastal areas has an adverse effect on the environment, coastal ecology and economics and hence, they cannot be permitted to operate. In Vijay Singh Puniya v. State of Rajasthan, the High Court of Rajasthan it was observed that any person who disturbs the ecological balance or degrades, pollutes and tinkers with the gifts of nature such as air, water, river, sea and other elements of the nature, he not only violates the fundamental right guaranteed under Art 21 of the Constitution, but also breaches the fundamental duty to protect the environment under Art 51A (g).

In Vellore Citizens' Welfare Forum vs. Union of India and Others[clxv], a three Judge Bench of this Court referred to these changes, to the `precautionary principle' and the new concept of `burden of proof' in environmental matters. Kuldip Singh, J. after referring to the principles evolved in various international Conferences and to the concept of `Sustainable Development', stated that the Precautionary Principle, the Polluter-Pays Principle and the special concept of Onus of Proof have now emerged and govern the law in our country too, as is clear from Articles 47, 48-A and 51-A(g) of our Constitution and that, in fact, in the various environmental statutes, such as the Water Act, 1974 and other statutes, including the Environment (Protection) Act, 1986, these concepts are already implied.

The relevant observations in the Vellore Case in this behalf read as follows:

"In view of the above-mentioned constitutional and statutory provisions we have no hesitation in holding that the Precautionary Principle and the Polluter Pays Principle are part of the environmental law of the country."

The Court observed that even otherwise the above- said principles are accepted as part of the Customary International Law and hence there should be no difficulty in accepting them as part of our domestic law. In fact on the facts of the case before this Court, it was directed that the authority to be appointed under section 3(3) of the Environment (Protection) Act, 1986 "shall implement the `Precautionary Principle' and the `Polluter Pays Principle'."

The learned Judges also observed that the new concept which places the Burden of Proof on the Developer or Industralist who is proposing to alter the status quo, has also become part of our environmental law.

The Vellore judgment has referred to these principles briefly but, in our view, it is necessary to explain their meaning in more detail, so that Courts and tribunals or environmental authorioties can properly apply the said principles in the matters which come before them.

This Court in explained the "Precautionary Principle" and "Polluters Pays principle" as under:-

Some of the salient principles of "Sustainable Development", as culled out from Brundtland Report and other international documents, are inter-Generational Equity, Use and Conservation of Natural Resources, Environmental Protection, the Precautionary Principle, Polluter Pays principle, Obligation to assist and cooperate, Eradication of Poverty and Financial Assistance to the developing countries. We are, however, of the view that "The Precautionary Principle" and "The Polluter Pays" principle are essential features of "Sustainable Development". The "Precautionary Principle" - in the context of the municipal law - means:

Environment measures - by the State Government and the statutory authorities - must anticipate, prevent and attack the causes of environmental degradation.

Where there are threats of serious and irreversible damage, lack of scientific certainty should not be used as a reason for postponing measures to prevent environmental degradation.

The "Onus of proof" is on the actor or the developer/industrialist to snow that this action is environmentally benign.

"The Polluter Pays" principle has been held to be a sound principle by this Court in Indian Council for *Enviro-Legal Action vs. Union of India* JT [clxvi]. The Court observed, "We are of the opinion that any principle evolved in this behalf should be simple, practical and suited to the conditions obtaining in this country". The Court ruled that "Once the activity carried on is hazardous or inherently dangerous, the person carrying on such activity is liable to make good the loss caused to any other person by his activity irrespective of the fact whether he took reasonable care while carrying on his activity. The rule is premised upon the very nature of the activity carried on".

Consequently the polluting industries are "absolutely liable to compensate for the harm caused by them to villagers in the affected area, to the soil and to the underground water and hence, they are bound to take all necessary measures to remove sludge and other pollutants lying in the affected areas". The "Polluter Pays" principle as interpreted by this Court means that the absolute liability for harm to the environment extends not only to compensate the victims of pollution but also the cost of restoring the environmental of the damaged environment is part of the process of "Sustainable Development" and as such polluter is liable to pay the cost to the individual sufferers as well as the cost of the reversing the damaged ecology The precautionary principle and the polluter pays principle have been accepted as part of the law of the land.

A.P. Pollution Control Board V. M.B. Nayudu[clxvii]it was held Article 21 which deals with both fundamental right to life and liberty. While environmental aspects concern `life', human rights aspects concern `liberty'. In our view, in the context of emerging jurisprudence relating to environmental matters, - as it is the case in matters relating to human rights, - it is the duty of this Court to render Justice by taking all aspects into consideration. With a view to ensure that there is neither danger to environment nor to ecology and at the same time ensuring sustainable development, this Court in our view, can refer scientific and technical aspects for investigation and opinion to expert bodies such as the Appellate Authority under the National Environmental Appellate Authority Act, 1997. The said authority comprises of a retired Judge of the Supreme Court and Members having technical expertise in environmental matters whose investigation, analysis of facts and opinion on objections raised by parties, could give adequate help to this Court or the High Courts and also the needed reassurance. Any opinions rendered by the said authority would of course be subject to the approval of this Court.

M.C. Mehta Vs. Union of India (UOI) and Ors.[clxviii] The main question to be examined in these matters is whether the mining activity in area upto 5 kilometers from the Delhi-Haryana border on the Haryana side of the ridge and also in the Aravalli hills causes environment degradation and what directions are required to be issued. The background in which the question has come up for
consideration may first be noticed. It has been suggested that the short term and long term action plan for the restoration of environmental quality of the area shall be prepared separately. The action plan shall be prepared in such a way that it should be a guiding tool also in the hands of the state
pollution control boards and Government agencies for enforcement of the environmental
laws for the restoration of environmental quality of the area. Monitoring programme shall
include frequency of monitoring for air quality, water quality, ground water, solid wastes,
noise level etc.
The court suggested a plan for conserving underground water, aforestation, stopping mining and for the preservation of flora and fauna in this case with the help of local population and government.

Conclusion
The pollution prevention guidelines give by the courts must be follower sincerely. All the environmental
upgradation measures need to be taken more seriously by public, government and the non- governmental organizations. There is need on the part of the State Government to immediately start these measures in the areas where degradation has already taken place. Right to pollution free environment has been recognized as a basic human right. Without a balanced and clean environment , right to life cannot be enjoyed in its fullest sense.

Essay- X

RIGHT TO HEALTH

The widely acceptable definition of health is that given by the WHO in the preamble of its constitution, according to World Health Organization, "Health is a state of complete physical, mental and social wellbeing and not merely the absence of disease."[clxix]

The enjoyment of the highest attainable standard of health is one of the fundamental rights of every human being without distinction of race, religion, political belief, economic or social condition. The health of all peoples is fundamental to the attainment of peace and security and is dependent upon the fullest co-operation of individuals and States.[clxx]

Current trends suggest that "the enjoyment of the highest attainable standard of health" which WHO describes as "one of the fundamental rights of every human being" is seen almost as a by-product, something that will trickle down to the bottom sometime in the future.

"The responsibility to respect, protect and fulfil the 'right to health' lies not only with the medical profession but also with public functionaries such as administrators and judges. In this context, the present programme is important since it seeks to highlight the inter- linkage between the promotion of healthcare and the language of human rights norms." [clxxi]

The traditional notion of healthcare has focused on aspects such as access to medical treatment, medicines and procedures. The field of professional ethics in the medical profession has accordingly dealt with the doctor-patient relationship and the expansion of facilities for curative treatment. Health care involves many factors like such as life-expectancy, mortality rates etc. The status of health of the individual depends upon various factors like societal level and the provision of nutrition, clothing and shelter, living environment, working conditions, education about disease-prevention and many other causes.

INTERNATIONAL HUMAN RIGHTS TO HEALTH

There is a foundational logic for health concerns to be addressed through the language of human rights. While professional ethics in the medical profession have retained an individual-centric focus on curative treatment, the evolution of international human rights norms pertaining to health has created a normative framework for governmental action.[clxxii]

The incorporation of health concerns in the 'rights' discourse, both at the international and domestic level – recognises that the legal system bears the responsibility of aiding the medical profession in advancing the 'right to health'. In fact, the onus on governmental agencies goes beyond aspects like the regulation of the medical profession and support for research and development (R&D) in the medical field. It also includes policy-choices pertaining to education,
housing, environmental protection, labour laws, social security provisions and the protection of intellectual property among others. Since the end of World War II, many such aspects have come to be recognised as part of a 'right to health' in international human rights.

In the context of international human rights, economic, social, and cultural rights are generally distinguished from civil and political rights. Although it is often asserted that both sets of rights are interdependent, interrelated, and of equal importance,' in practice, Western states and NGOs, in particular, have tended to treat economic, social, and cultural rights as if they were less important than civil and political rights.

It has been argued that the term "right to health" is awkward because it suggests that people have a right to something that cannot be guaranteed, namely perfect health or to be healthy. It has also been noted that health is a highly subjective matter, varying from person to person and from country to country. It is argued, therefore, that the terms "right to healthcare" or "right to health protection" are more realistic.

At the international level, however, the term "right to health" is most commonly used. This term best matches the international human rights treaty provisions that formulate health as a human right. These provisions not only proclaim a right to healthcare but also a right to other health services such as environmental health protection and occupational health services. The term "healthcare" would accordingly not cover this broader understanding of health as a human right. Thus, in practice the term "right to health" is generally used as a shorthand expression for the more elaborate treaty texts. Using such shorthand expressions is rather common in human rights discourse; terms such as the rights to life, privacy, a fair trial, and housing have all obtained a very specific practical connotation, as has the right to health.

INTERNATIONAL CONVENTIONS

The evolution towards defining health as a social issue led to the founding of the World Health Organization (WHO) in 1946.[clxxiii] With the emergence of health as a public issue, the conception of health changed. WHO developed and promulgated the understanding of health as "a state of complete physical, mental and social well-being and not merely the absence of disease or infirmity." [clxxiv] It defined an integrated approach linking together all the factors related to human well-being, including physical and social surroundings conducive to good health.

With the establishment of WHO, for the first time the right to health was recognized internationally. The WHO Constitution affirms that "the enjoyment of the highest attainable standard of health is one of the fundamental rights of every human being without distinction of race, religion, political belief, economic or social condition."

Universal recognition of the right to health was further confirmed in the 1978 Declaration of Alma-Ata on Primary Health Care, in which states pledged to progressively develop comprehensive health care systems to ensure effective and equitable distribution of resources for maintaining health. They reiterated their responsibility to provide for the health of their populations, " which can be fulfilled only by the provision of adequate health and social measures."[clxxv]The Declaration develops the bases for implementing primary health care systems, which have implications for the observance of the right. While this instrument is not binding, it does represent a further commitment on the part of states in respect of the right to health, and establishes the framework for an integrated policy aimed at securing its enjoyment.

Various U.N treaties intend to protect right to health also with other human rights, these include UN human rights treaties . Convention on the

Elimination of All Forms of Discrimination Against Women (CEDAW), 1979[clxxvi] . Regional human rights treaties include European Social Charter, 1961 , African Charter on Human and Peoples' Rights, 1981 , Additional Protocol to the American Convention on Human Rights in the Area of Economic, Social and Cultural Rights (the Protocol of San Salvador), 1988. The 1989 Convention on the Rights of the Child: art. 24. The 1990 International Convention on the Protection of the Rights of All Migrant Workers and Members of Their Families: Arts. 28, 43 (e) and 45 (c) , The 2006 Convention on the Rights of Persons with Disabilities: Art. 25.

The International Covenant on Economic, Social and Cultural Rights (1966) in Article 12 [clxxvii] states steps for the realization of the right to health include step to reduce infant mortality and ensure the healthy development of the child; step to improve environmental and industrial hygiene; step to prevent, treat and control epidemic, endemic, occupational and other diseases; and step to create conditions to ensure access to health care for all.

To clarify and operationalize the above provisions, the UN Committee on Economic, Social and Cultural Rights which monitors compliance with the ICESCR adopted a General Comment on the Right to Health in 2000. The General Comment sets out that the right to health extends not only to timely and appropriate health care but also to the underlying determinants of health, such as access to safe and potable water and adequate sanitation, an adequate supply of safe food, nutrition and housing, healthy occupational and environmental conditions and access to health-related education and information, including on sexual and reproductive health.

According to the General Comment the right to health contains four elements: Availability. Functioning public health and health care facilities, goods and services, as well as programmes in sufficient quantity. Accessibility: Health facilities, goods and services accessible to everyone, within the jurisdiction of the State party. Accessibility has four overlapping dimensions: Acceptability: All health facilities, goods and services must be respectful of medical ethics and culturally appropriate, as well as sensitive to gender and life-cycle requirements. Quality: Health facilities, goods and services must be scientifically and medically appropriate and of good quality. According to the General Comment, the right to health also has a "core content" referring to the minimum essential level of the right

States Parties are expected to take steps forward in conformity with the principle of progressive realization. This imposes an obligation to move forward as expeditiously and effectively as possible, individually and through international assistance and co-operation, to the maximum of available resources.

Numerous conferences and declarations, such as the International Conference on Primary Health Care (resulting in the Declaration of Alma-Ata), the United Nations Millennium Declaration and Millennium Development Goals, and the Declaration of Commitment on HIV/AIDS, have also helped clarify various aspects of public health relevant to the right to health and have reaffirmed commitments to its realization.

Declaration of Alma-Ata, 1978 The Declaration affirms the crucial role of primary health care, which addresses the main health problems in the community, providing promotive, preventive, curative and rehabilitative services accordingly (art. VII). It stresses that access to primary health care is the key to attaining a level of health that will permit all individuals to lead a socially and economically productive life (art. V) and to contributing to the realization of the highest attainable standard of health.

The right to health is also recognized in several regional instruments, such as the African Charter on Human and Peoples' Rights (1981), the Additional Protocol to the American Convention on Human Rights in the Area of Economic, Social and Cultural Rights, known as the Protocol of San Salvador (1988), and the European Social Charter (1961, revised in 1996). The American Convention on Human Rights (1969) and the European Convention for the Promotion of Human Rights and Fundamental Freedoms (1950) contain provisions related to health, such as the right to life, the prohibition on torture and other cruel, inhuman and degrading treatment, and the right to family and private life.

Finally, the right to health or the right to health care is recognized in at least 115 constitutions. At least six other constitutions set out duties in relation to health, such as the duty on the State to develop health services or to allocate a specific budget to them.

Constitution of India

Article 38 of Indian Constitution imposes liability on State that states will secure a social order for the promotion of welfare of the people but without public health we cannot achieve it. It means without public health welfare of people is impossible. Article 39(e) related with workers to protect their health. Article 41 imposed duty on State to public assistance basically for those who are sick and disable. Article 42 makes provision to protect the health of infant and mother by maternity benefit.

In the India the Directive Principle of State Policy under the Article

47 considers it the primary duty of the state to improve public health, securing of justice, human condition of works, extension of sickness, old age, disablement and maternity benefits and also contemplated. Further, State's duty includes prohibition of consumption of intoxicating drinking and drugs are injurious to health. Article 48A ensures that State shall Endeavour to protect and impose the pollution free environment for good health.

Article 47 makes improvement of public health a primary duty of State. Hence, the court should enforce this duty against a defaulting authority on pain of penalty prescribe by law, regardless of the financial resources of such authority.

Under Article 47, the State shall regard the raising of the level of nutrition and standard of living of its people and improvement of public health as among its primary duties. None of these lofty ideals can be achieved without controlling pollution inasmuch as our materialistic resources are limited and the claimants are many.

The Food Corporation of India being an agency of the State must conform to the letter and spirit of Article 47 to improve public health it should not allow sub-standard food grains to reach the public market. The State under Article 47 has to protect poverty stricken people who are consumer of sub-standard food from injurious effects.

This Directive Principle has now been translated into action through the 73rd Amendment Act 1992 whereby part IX of the constitution titled "The Panchayats" was inserted. The Panchayat system has significant implications for the health sector. There will be discussed in relation to relevant Articles 243-243A to 243O contained in Part IX. Panchayat, Municipalities liable to improve and protect public health. Article 243G says 'State that the legislature of a state may endow the panchayats with necessary power and authority in relation to matters listed in the eleventh Schedule". The entries in this schedule having direct relevance to health are as follows:

11 -Drinking

23 -Health and sanitation including hospitals, primary health centers and dispensaries.

24 -Family welfare

25 -Women and Child development

26 -Social welfare including welfare of the handicapped and mentally retarded.

Article 243-W finds place in part IXA of the constitution titled "The

Municipalities:

5 -Water supply for domestic industrial and commercial purpose.

6 -Public health, sanitation conservancy and solid waste management.

9 -Safeguarding the interest of weaker sections of society, including the handicapped and mentally retarded.

16 -Vital statistics including registration of births and deaths

17- Regulation of slaughter – houses and tanneries.

Article 41 provides right to assistance in case of sickness and disablement. It deals with "The state shall within the limits of its economic capacity and development, make effective provisions for securing the right to work, to education and to public assistance in case of unemployment, Old age, sickness and disablement and in other cases of undeserved want". Their implications in relation to health are obvious. Article 42 give the power to State for make provision for securing just and humane conditions of work and for maternity relief and for the protection of environment same as given by Article 48A and same obligation impose to Indian citizen by Article 51A.(g).

Judicial Response

In a series of cases dealing with the substantive content of the right to life, the court has found that the right live with human dignity including right to good health.

In Consumer Education and Research Center v. UOI], the Court explicitly held that the right to health was an integral factor of a meaningful right to life. The court held that the right to health and medical care is a fundamental right under Article 21. The Supreme Court, while examining the issue of the constitutional right to health care under arts 21, 41 and 47 of the Constitution of India.

The DPSP are only the directives to the State. These are non-justifiable. No person can claim for non-fulfilling these directives. But the Supreme Court has brought the right to health under the preview of Article 21. The scope of this provision is very wide. It prescribes for the right of life and personal liberty. The concept of personal liberty comprehended many rights, related to indirectly to life or liberty of a person. And now a person can claim his right of health. Thus, the right to health, along with numerous other civil, political and economic rights, is afforded protection under the Indian Constitution.

The Constitution guarantees the some fundamental rights having a bearing on health care. Article 21deal with "No person shall be deprived of his life or personal liberty except according to procedure established by law." Right to live means something more, than more animal existence and includes the right to live consistently with human dignity and decency.

In 1995, the Supreme Court held that right to health and medical care is a fundamental right covered by Article 21 since health is essential for making the life of workmen meaningful and purposeful and compatible with personal dignity. The state has an obligation under Article 21 to safeguard the right to life of every person, preservation of human life being of paramount importance. The Supreme Court has in the case of *Parmanand Katra vs Union of India* [clxxviii] Apex Court observed "There can be no second opinion that preservation of human life is of paramount importance. That is so on account of the fact that once life is lost, the status quo ante cannot be restored as resurrection is beyond the capacity of man. The patient whether he be an innocent person or be a criminal liable to punishment under the laws of the society, it is the obligation of those who are in charge of the health of the community to preserve life so that the innocent may be protected and the guilty may be punished. Social laws do not contemplate death by negligence to tantamount to legal punishment.
 Article 21 of the Constitution casts the obligation on the State to preserve life. The provision as explained by this Court in scores of decisions has emphasised and reiterated with gradually increasing emphasis that position. A doctor at the Government hospital positioned to meet this State obligation is, therefore, duty bound to extend medical assistance for preserving life. Every doctor whether at a Government hospital or otherwise has the professional obligation to extend his services with due expertise for protecting life. No law or State action can intervene to avoid/delay the discharge of the paramount obligation cast upon members of the medical profession. The obligation being total, absolute and paramount, laws of procedure whether in statutes or otherwise which would interfere with the discharge of this obligation cannot be sustained and must, therefore, give way."

The Supreme Court in this case ruled that every doctor whether at a Government hospital or otherwise has the professional obligation to extend his services with due expertise for protecting life. No law or state action can intervene to avoid delay, the discharge of the paramount obligation cast upon members of the medical profession. The obligation being total, absolute, and paramount, laws of procedure whether in statutes or otherwise which would interfere with the discharge of this obligation cannot be sustained, and must, therefore, give way. The Court laid down the following guidelines for doctors, when an injured person approaches them:

Duty of a doctor when an injured person approaches him: Whenever, on such occasions, a man of the medical profession is approached by an injured person, and if he finds that whatever assistance he could give is not really sufficient to save the life of the person, but some better assistance is necessary, it is the duty of the man in the medical profession so approached to render all the help which he could, and also see that the person reaches the proper expert as early as possible.

Legal protection to doctors treating injured persons: A doctor does not contravene the law of the land by proceeding to treat an injured victim on his appearance before him, either by himself or with others. Zonal regulations and classifications cannot operate as fetters in the discharge of the obligation, even if the victim is sent elsewhere under local rules, and regardless of the involvement of police. The 1985 decision of the Standing Committee on Forensic Medicine is the effective guideline

No legal bar on doctors from attending to the injured persons: There is no legal impediment for a medical professional, when he is called upon or requested to attend to an injured person needing his medical assistance immediately. The effort to save the person should be the top priority, not only of the medical professional, but even of the police or any other citizen who happens to be connected with the matter, or who happens to notice such an incident or a situation.

The Supreme Court, in *Paschim Banga Khet mazdoor Samity & ors v. State of West Bengal & ors*[lxxix] Court in the context of medico-legal cases. has emphasized the need for rendering immediate medical aid to injured persons to preserve life and the obligations of the State as well as doctors in that regard. This petition filed under Article 32 of the Constitution raises this issue in the context of availability of facilities in Government-hospitals for treatment of persons sustaining serious injuries. While widening the scope of art 21 and the government's responsibility to provide medical aid to every person in the country, held that in a welfare state, the primary duty of the government is to secure the welfare of the people. Providing adequate medical facilities for the people is an obligation undertaken by the government in a welfare state. The government discharges this obligation by providing medical care to the persons seeking to avail of those facilities.

Article 21 imposes an obligation on the state to safeguard the right to life of every person. Preservation of human life is thus of paramount importance. The government hospitals run by the state are duty bound to extend medical assistance for preserving human life. Failure on the part of a government hospital to provide timely medical treatment to a person in need of such treatment, results in violation of his right to life guaranteed under Article21. The Court made certain additional direction in respect of serious medical cases:

- Adequate facilities be provided at the public health canters where the patient can be given basic treatment and his condition stabilized.
- Hospitals at the district and sub divisional level should be upgraded so that serious cases be treated there.
- Facilities for given specialist treatment should be increased and having regard to the growing needs, it must be made available at the district and sub divisional level hospitals.
- In order to ensure availability of bed in any emergency at State level hospitals, there should be a centralized communication system so that the patient can be sent immediately to the hospital where bed is available in respect of the treatment, which is required.
- Proper arrangement of ambulance should be made for transport of a patient from the public health center to the State hospital.
- Ambulance should be adequately provided with necessary equipments and medical personnel.

The Supreme Court has recognized the rights of the workers and their right to basic health facilities under the Constitution, as well as under the international conventions to which India is a party. In its path breaking judgment in *Bandhua Mukti Morcha v Union of India*,[clxxx] the court delineated the scope of art 21 of the Constitution, and held that it is the fundamental right of every one in this country, assured under the interpretation given to art 21 by this court in Francis Mullin's Case to live with human dignity, free from exploitation. This right to live with human dignity enshrined in art 21 derives its life breath from the directive principles of state policy and particularly clause (e) and (f) of art 39 and arts 41 and 42. It must include protection of the health and strength of workers, men and women; and children of tender age against abuse; opportunities and facilities for children to develop in a healthy manner and in conditions of freedom and dignity; educational facilities; just and humane conditions of work and maternity relief. These are the minimum requirements, which must exist in order to enable a person to live with human dignity. No state, neither the central government nor any state government, has the right to take any action which will deprive a person of the enjoyment of these basic essentials.

In the case of *A.S Mittal v State of Uttar Pradesh* [clxxxi] public interest litigation brought under article 32 of the constitutions and the allied negligence on the part of the doctors in a free eye care camp at Khurja. However laudable the intentions with which it might it have been launched. The operated eyes of the patient were irreversibly damaged owing to post-operative infection. The mishap was due to some common contaminated source. After an inquiry it was found that it was due to normal saline used in the eyes at the time of the operation. The vision of 84 persons could not be restored. The court held that a mistake by a medical practitioner, which no reasonably competent and careful practitioner would have committed, is a negligent one. The court further held that the highest standard of aseptic and sterile should be maintained. The govt. spends so much on public health but standard of cleanliness and hygiene are to be desired. The victims were given a compensation of Rs 5000 as interim relief. The state govt. was directed to pay a sum of Rs. 12,500 to each of the victim.

In *Common cause v. Union of India*,[clxxxii] Supreme Court highlighted the serious deficiencies and shortcomings in the matter of collection, shortage and supply of blood through various blood centres operating in the country, especially in the context of H.I.V. infected people.

In *Mr X v. Hospital Z*[clxxxiii] it was concluded by the Supreme Court that right of privacy cannot be treated be an absolute right and in paragraph 26, the Supreme Court provided the following important guidelines. It was held that as one of the basic Human Rights, the right of privacy is not treated as absolute and is subject to such action as may be lawfully taken for the prevention of crime or disorder or protection of health or morals or protection of rights and freedoms of others.

Conclusion

It is necessary that the various catagories of factors on which the right to health depends e.g. health services, safe working conditions, adequate housing and nutritious foods should be improved. Achieving the right to health is closely related to that of other human rights, including the right to food, housing, work. Therefore violations or lack of attention to human rights can have serious health consequences. Discrimination in the delivery of health services violates fundamental human rights. Equal attention should be given to the vulnerable and marginalized groups of the society. There is a need of a human rights-based approach to health and to frame the strategies and solutions to end the discriminatory practices which are often the basic reasons of violation of right to health. Human rights-based approach should be followed at the Union as well as state levels which should be targeted to frame all health policies, strategies and programmes with the objective of progressively improving the enjoyment of all people to the right to health.

Essay-XI

RIGHTS OF PRISONERS

Oscar Wilde says :

"*Every prison that men build is built with bricks of shame and bound with bars, lest Christ should see, how men, their brothers maim*".

Life in prison is not the same as in the free world. It is necessary to put constraints on freedom in social interest. Criminals are kept separate in order to keep them segregated from the community to prevent them from repeating crime again and reforming them and in some cases in order to deter people. The basic object of Criminal Law is to suppress crime. Society must be protected from transgressions of Law.

Imprisonment involving denial of liberty of the individual signifies the societal disapproval of the
violation of law by him. As such it cannot be denied that it has some punitive content and the system expects the prisoner to suffer some disabilities including his freedom of movement. Therefore one cannot expect the state of life in prison to be the same as in the free world. Restrict
ions on freedom are inevitable. Despite this position the system cannot ignore the fact that a prisoner is also a human being. Basic necessities of a human being should not be denied to him.

The poor, illiterate and weaker sections in our society in our country suffer day in and day out in their struggle for survival and look to those who have promised them equality- social, political and economic...a very large number of under–trial prisoners suffer prolonged incarceration even in petty criminal matters merely for the reason that they are not in a position, even in bailable offences, to furnish bail bonds and get released on bail." clxxxiv

The law should strive to strike a balance between these equally competing interests. The present state of affairs in prisons are not conducive to strike this balance. The pathetic conditions of prisoners are not confined to India alone. This can be seen every where throughout the world.clxxxv

Prisoners also human beings, they should have rights as every person alive has at the very least, the inaleinable rights to life, liberty, and the pursuit of happiness. One may think that being a prisoner negates the right to liberty, but on the contrary it is an example of the consequences of using one's right to liberty. Many people, sometimes argue that prisoners don't have or should not be allowed to enjoy their human rights. Such arguments have no basis in law. Prisoners are human being and as such they retain their rights even when in prison. A person becomes a prisoner because of his conduct in conflict with the law. But he should not be denied of all the rights because human rights are universal. This means that every person, including a prisoner, has human rights, no matter who he is, where he lives or what is his race, sex, age, social status, etc.

This is also true that no right is absolute. This means that the enjoyment of human rights may be restricted or limited in certain circumstances. For example, all people have the right to liberty, the right to practice any profession, occupation, trade or business, the right to freedom of movement, etc. But these rights cannot be given to a prisoner. Such restrictions or limitations are lawful and in conformity with the legal norms.
They have rights like right of non discrimination, food, health and the right to dignity, the right not be tortured or treated cruelly or inhumanely etc.

International human rights law

International human rights law is binding on all States and their agents, including prison officials.
Human rights are a legitimate subject for international law and international scrutiny.
Law enforcement officials are obliged to know, and to apply, international standards for human rights.

Basic Principles for the Treatment of Prisoners

Adopted and proclaimed by General Assembly resolution 45/111 of 14 December 1990

1. All prisoners shall be treated with the respect due to their inherent dignity and value as human beings.

2. There shall be no discrimination on the grounds of race, colour, sex, language, religion, political or other opinion, national or social origin, property, birth or other status.

3. It is, however, desirable to respect the religious beliefs and cultural precepts of the group to which prisoners belong, whenever local conditions so require.

4. The responsibility of prisons for the custody of prisoners and for the protection of society against crime shall be discharged in keeping with a State's other social objectives and its fundamental responsibilities for promoting the well-being and development of all members of society.

5. Except for those limitations that are demonstrably necessitated by the fact of incarceration, all prisoners shall retain the human rights and fundamental freedoms set out in the Universal Declaration of Human Rights, and, where the State concerned is a party, the International Covenant on Economic, Social and Cultural Rights, and the International Covenant on Civil and Political Rights and the Optional Protocol thereto, as well as such other rights as are set out in other United Nations covenants.

6. All prisoners shall have the right to take part in cultural activities and education aimed at the full development of the human personality.

7. Efforts addressed to the abolition of solitary confinement as a punishment, or to the restriction of its use, should be undertaken and encouraged.

8. Conditions shall be created enabling prisoners to undertake meaningful remunerated employment which will facilitate their reintegration into the country's labour market and permit them to contribute to their own financial support and to that of their families.

9. Prisoners shall have access to the health services available in the country

without discrimination on the grounds of their legal situation.

10. With the participation and help of the community and social institutions, and with due regard to the interests of victims, favourable conditions shall be created for the reintegration of the ex-prisoner into society under the best possible conditions.

International Covenant on Civil and Political Rights

The International Covenant on Civil and Political Rights came into force 23 March 1976. Article 10 of the International Covenant on Civil and Political Rights provides that any person deprived of their liberty shall be treated with humanity and dignity. The article imposes a requirement of separation of prisoners in pre-trial detention from those already convicted of crimes, as well as a specific obligation to separate accused juvenile prisoners from adults and bring them before trial speedily. There is also a requirement that the focus of prisons should be reform and rehabilitation, not punishment. These provisions apply to those in prisons, hospitals (particularly psychiatric hospitals), detention facilities, correction facilities or any other facility in which a person is deprived of their liberty. The article complements article 7 of the Covenant, which bans torture or other cruel, inhumane or degrading treatment, by guaranteeing those deprived of their liberty with the same conditions as that set for free persons.

UN Standard Minimum Rules for the Treatment of Prisoners[clxxxvi]

The UN Standard Minimum Rules for the Treatment of Prisoners came into force in 1955.[clxxxvii] The standards set out by the UN are not legally binding but offer guidelines in international and municipal law with respect to any person held in any form of custody. They are generally regarded as being good principle and practice for the management of custodial facilities. The document sets out standards for those in custody which covers registration, personal hygiene, clothing and bedding, food, exercise and sport, medical services, discipline and punishment, instruments of restraint, information to and complaints by prisoners, contact with the outside world, books, religion, retentions of prisoners' property, notification of death, illness, transfer, removal of prisoners, institutional personnel and inspection of facilities. It also sets out guidelines for prisoners under sentence which further includes treatment, classification and individualisation, privileges, work, educations and recreations, and social relations and after-care. There are also special provisions for insane and mentally abnormal prisoners, prisoners under arrest or awaiting trial, civil prisoners and persons arrested or detained without charge. Standard Minimum Rules for the Treatment of Prisoners Adopted by the First United Nations Congress on the Prevention of Crime and the Treatment of Offenders, held at Geneva in 1955, and approved by the Economic and Social Council by its resolutions 663 C (XXIV) of 31 July 1957 and 2076 (LXII) of 13 May 1977 These rules are not intended to describe in detail a model system of penal institutions. They seek only, on the basis of the general consensus of contemporary thought and the essential elements of the most adequate systems of today, to set out what is generally accepted as being good principle and practice in the treatment of prisoners and the management of institutions. They represent, as a whole, the minimum conditions which are accepted as suitable by the United Nations. On the other hand, the rules cover a field in which thought is constantly developing. They are not intended to preclude experiment and practices, provided these are in harmony with the principles and seek to further the purposes which derive from the text of the rules as a whole. It will always be justifiable for the central prison administration to authorize departures from the rules in this spirit. Part I of the rules covers the general management of institutions, and is applicable to all categories of prisoners, criminal or civil, untried or convicted, including prisoners subject to "security measures" or corrective measures ordered by the judge. The rules provide that there shall be no discrimination on grounds of race, colour, sex, language, religion, political or other opinion, national or social origin, property, birth or other status, it is necessary to respect the religious beliefs and moral precepts of the group to which a prisoner belongs. The different categories of prisoners shall be kept in separate institutions or parts of institutions taking account of their sex, age, criminal record, the legal reason for their detention and the necessities of their treatment. Thus, Men and women shall so far as possible be detained in separate institutions; in an institution which receives both men and women the whole of the premises allocated to women shall be entirely separate; Untried prisoners shall be kept separate from convicted prisoners;) Persons imprisoned for debt and other civil prisoners shall be kept separate from persons imprisoned by reason of a criminal offence; Young prisoners shall be kept separate from adults.

Children are to benefit from all the human rights and guarantees available to adults. In addition, the rules are also applied to children: Children who are detained shall be treated in a manner which promotes their sense of dignity and worth, facilitates their reintegration into society, reflects their best interests and takes their needs into account. Children shall not be subjected to corporal punishment, capital punishment or life imprisonment without possibility of release. Children who are detained shall be separated from adult prisoners. Accused juveniles shall be separated from adults and brought for trial as speedily as possible. Special efforts shall be made to allow detained children to receive visits from and correspond with family members. The privacy of a detained child shall be respected, and complete and secure records are to be maintained and kept confidential. Juveniles of compulsory school age have the right to education and to vocational training. Weapons shall not be carried in institutions which hold juveniles. Disciplinary procedures shall respect the child's dignity and be designed to instil in the child a sense of justice, self-respect and respect for human rights. Parents are to be notified of the admission, transfer, release, sickness, injury or death of a juvenile.

European Convention for the Prevention of Torture and Inhuman or Degrading Treatment or Punishment

The European Convention for the Prevention of Torture and Inhuman or Degrading Treatment or Punishment entered into force on 1 March 2002.¹ The Convention establishes the European Committee for the Prevention of Torture and Inhuman or Degrading Treatment or Punishment (the Committee). The Committee is permitted to visit all places of detention, defined by the convention as "any place within its jurisdiction where persons are deprived of their liberty by a public authority."Once a state government is notified of the intention of the Committee to carry out a visit it is required to allow access to the territory with the right to free travel without restriction, full information of the facility in question, unlimited access to the facility and free movement within it, the right to interview any person being held within the facility, communicate freely with any person whom it believes can supply relevant information and access to any other information which the Committee feels is necessary to carry out its task. All information gathered is confidential. In exceptional circumstances a state may make representations based on grounds of national defence, public safety, serious disorder in custodial facilities against a visit to a certain place or at a certain time. After each visit a report is drawn up with any possible suggestions to the state in question.

Convention on the Rights of Persons with Disabilities

The Convention on the Rights of Persons with Disabilities entered into force on 30 March 2007 and has 154 state parties. The Convention's purpose is to "promote, protect and ensure the full and equal enjoyment of all human rights and fundamental freedoms by all persons with disabilities, and to promote respect for their inherent dignity."Persons with disabilities are defined as those "who have long-term physical, mental, intellectual or sensory impairments which in interaction with various barriers may hinder their full and effective participation in society on an equal basis with others.""Article 13 of the Convention relates to access to justice for persons with disability. It provides that in order to "ensure effective access to justice for persons with disabilities, States Parties shall promote appropriate training for those working in the field of administration of justice, including police and prison staff."

Prisons in India

Prisons and their administration in India is a state subject covered by item 4 under the State List in the Seventh Schedule of the Constitution of India. The management and administration of prisons falls exclusively in the domain of the State governments, and is governed by the Prisons Act, 1894 and the Prison manuals of the respective state governments. Thus, states have the primary role, responsibility and authority to change the current prison laws, rules and regulations. The Central Government provides assistance to the states to improve security in prisons, for the repair and renovation of old prisons, medical facilities, development of borstal schools, facilities to women offenders, vocational training, modernization of prison industries, training to prison personnel, and for the creation of high security enclosures.

In India, eighty percent of the inmates in the jails are under trials. The major problems faced by these inmates are not only of not getting a trial but that of not being granted bail, inhuman treatment in jails, facing poor conditions, lack of proper medical treatment, etc. There are various statutes such as the Prisoners Act, 1894; the Model Manual Prison India, etc. and various precedents which have been laid down in landmark cases which provide for the rights which these prisoners are entitled to. However, the problem today lies not in the availability of these rights but in the implementation of these rights and precedents.[clxxxviii] Under the Prisoners Rights non-goverrnental organizations are also working towards helping these prisoners get their rightful treatment in the prisons, safeguard their access to a fair and speedy trial, facilitate bail procedures and work towards various other procedural requirements to ensure that these prisoners make efforts to only achieve reformation and don't have to fight for their survival.

Judicial Appproach-

The Supreme Court of India, in its judgments on various aspects of prison administration, has laid down the basic principles regarding imprisonment and custody. Resultantly this has been established that a person in prison does not become a non-person and he is entitled to all human rights within the limitations of imprisonment. .

In, *N. H.Hoskot v. Maharashtra,* [clxxxix] It was laid down that it is implicit in the power of the court to deprive the sentence of his personal liberty, the Court has to ensure that no more and noless than is warranted by the sentence happens. If the prisoner breaks down because of mental torture, psychic pressure or physical infliction beyond the licit limits of lawful imprisonment the Prison Administration shall be liable for the excess. On the contrary, if an influential convict is able to buy advantages and liberties to avoid or water down the deprivation implied in the sentence the Prison Establishment will be called to order for such adulteration or dilution of court sentences by executive palliation, if unwarranted by law.

In *Sunil Batra v. Delhi Administration*[cxc] The petitioner, a convict under death sentence, through
a letter to one of the Judges of this Court alleged that torture was practiced upon another prisoner by a jail warder, to extract money from the victim through his visiting relations. The letter was converted into a habeas corpus proceeding. The Court issued notice to the State and the concerned officials. It also appointed amicus curiae and authorised them to visit the prison, meet the prisoner, see relevant documents and interview necessary witnesses so as
to enable them to inform themselves about the surrounding circumstances and the scenario of events.

The amicus curiae after visiting the jail and examining witnesses reported that the prisoner sustained serious anal injury because a rod was driven into that aperture to inflict inhuman torture and that as the bleeding had not stopped, he was removed to the jail hospital and later to
the Irvin Hospital. It was also reported that the prisoner's explanation for the anal rupture was an unfulfilled demand of thewarder for money.
The court found violation of Art. 21of the Constitution and commented, "Prisons are built with stones of law' and so it beholds the court to insist that, in the eye of law, prisoners are persons, not animals, and punish the deviant 'guardians' of the prison system where they go berserk and defile the dignity of the human inmate. Prison houses are part of Indian earth and the Indian Constitution cannot be held at bay by jail officials 'dressed ill a little, brief authority', when Part III is invoked by a convict. For when a prisoner is traumatized, the Constitution suffers a shock. And when the Court takes cognizance of such violence and violation, it does, like the. Hound of Heaven."
It was held that no solitary or punitive cell, no hard labour or dietary change as painful additive, no other punishment or denial of privileges and amenities, no transfer to other prisons with penal consequences, shall be imposed without judicial appraisal of the Sessions Judge and where such intimation,

on account of emergency, is difficult, such information shall be given within two days of the action.

The direction was given that the State shall take early steps to prepare in Hindi, a Prisoner's Handbook and circulate copies to bring legal awareness home to the inmates. Periodical jail bulletins stating how improvements and habilitative programmes are brought into the prison may create a fellow-ship which will ease tensions. A prisoners' wall paper, which will freely ventilate grievances will also reduce stress. All these are implementary of s. 61 of the Prisons Act.

Direction was given that State shall take steps to keep up to the Standard Minimum Rules for Treatment of Prisoners recommended by the United Nations, especially those relating to work and wages, treatment with dignity community contact and correctional strategies.

The Court commented that The Prisons Act needs rehabilitation and the Prison Manual total overhaul, even the Model Manual being out of focus with healing goals. A correctional-cum orientation course is necessitous for the prison staff inculcating the constitutional values, therapeutic approaches and tension- free management.

It was also directed that the prisoners' rights shall be protected by the court by its writ jurisdiction plus contempt power. To make this jurisdiction viable, free legal services to the prisoner programmes shall be promoted by professional organisations recognised by the Court such as for e.g. Free Legal Aid (Supreme Court) Society. The District Bar shall, we re-commend, keep a cell for prisoner relief. In this connection, it is heartening to note that the Delhi University, Faculty of Law, has a scheme of free legal assistance even to prisoners.

In, *State of Maharashtra v.Prabhakar*,[cxci] court examined rule 30 and Bombay Conditions of Detention Order, 1951.A Book was written by detenu in jail. He made a request to send it out of jail for publication. The question was whether the State Government can refuse request. It was held that the said conditions regulating the restrictions on the personal liberty of a detenu arc not privileges conferred on him, but are the conditions subject to which his liberty can be restricted. As there is no condition in the Bombay Conditions of Detention Order, 1951, prohibiting a detenu from writing a book or sending it for publication, the State of Maharashtra infringed the personal liberty of the first respondent in derogation of the law whereunder he is detained. The appellant, therefore, acted contrary to law in refusing to send the manuscript book of the detenu out of the jail to his wife for eventual publication.

In *Sunil Batra v. Delhi Administration* [cxcii] Apex Court rejected the 'hands-off' doctrine and ruled that fundamental rights do not flee the person as he enters the prison although they may suffer shrinkage necessitated by incarceration. The court explained that the judicial process casts the convict into the prison system and the deprivation of his freedom is not a blind penitentiary affliction but a belighted institutionalisation geared to a social good. The court has a continuing responsibility to ensure that the constitutional purpose of the deprivation is not defeated by the prison administration. It was held that both whether inside prison or outside, a person shall not be deprived of his guaranteed freedom save by methods 'right, just and fair'. A prisoner wears the armour of basic freedom even behind bars and that on breach thereof by lawless officials the law will respond to his distress signals through 'writ' aid.

In, *A Convict Prisoner In the Central Prison Vs. State of Kerala* [cxciii], the court held that absence of resources will be no justification for failing to secure humane conditions in prison. Institutional reform litigations must be put on a higher pedestal. Where Government has a constitutional obligation, it cannot plead want of funds, in excuse for not discharging its sovereign functions.

In *Charles Sobraj Vs. Superintendent Central Jail, Tihar, New Delhi* [cxciv], The petitioner a convict having to serve two sentences of long imprisonment, plus record of one escape and one attempt of suicide and interpol. reports of many crimes abroad in addition to several cases pending in India against him, through this writ petition contended that barbarity and inhuman treatment have been hurled at him and that intentional discrimination has been his lot throughout and, therefore sought the assistance or this Court for directing the jail authorities to give him finer foreigner as companions, and to remove him from a high security ward. It was held that whenever fundamental rights are flouted or legislative protection ignored to any prisoner's prejudice, this Court's writ will run breaking through stone walls and iron bars, to right the wrong and restore the rule of law. It was explained that Art. 21 of the Constitution read with Art. 19(1)(d) and (5) is capable of wider application than the imperial mischief which give its birth and must draw its meaning from the evolving standards of decency and dignity that mark the progress of a mature society. Fair procedure is the soul of Art. 21,

reasonableness of the restriction is the essence of Art. 19(5) and sweeping discretion degenerating into
arbitrary discrimination is anthema for Art. 14.
Constitutional Karuna is thus injected into incarceratory strategy to produce prison justice.

In *Francis Coralie Mullin Vs. Union Territory of Delhi & Ors.*[cxcv] a Right of the detenu under Conservation of Foreign Exchange & Prevention of Smuggling Activities Act, to have interview with a lawyer and the members of his family was under consideration. It was held that the power of preventive detention has been recognised as a necessary evil and is tolerated in a free
society in the larger interest of security of the State and maintenance of public order. It is a drastic power to detain a person without trial
and in many countries it is not allowed to be exercised except in times of war or aggression. The Indian Constitution does recognise the existence of this power, but it is hedged-in by various safeguards set out in Articles 21 and 22. Article 22 in clauses (4) to (7) deals specifically with safeguards
against preventive detention and enjoins that any law of preventive detention or action by way of preventive detention taken
under such law must be in conformity with
the restrictions laid down by those clauses on pain of invalidation, Article 21 also lays down restrictions on the power of preventive detention. It was held that Article 21 as interpreted in Maneka Gandhi's case requires that no one shall be deprived of his life or personal liberty except by procedure established by law and this procedure must be reasonable, fair and just and not arbitrary, whimsical or fanciful and it is for the Court to decide in the exercise of its constitutional power or judicial review whether the deprivation of life or personal liberty in a given case is by procedure, which is
reasonable, fair and just or it is otherwise. The law of preventive detention must, therefore, pass the test not only of Article 22 but also of Article 21. But, despite these safeguards laid down by the Constitution and creatively evolved by the Courts. the power of preventive detention is
a frightful and awesome power with drastic consequences
affecting personal liberty, which is the most cherished and prized possession of man in a civilised society. It is a power to be exercised with the greatest care and caution and
the courts have to be ever vigilant to see that this power is not abused or misused, inasmuch as the preventive detention is qualitatively different from punitive detention

and their purposes are different. In case of punitive detention, the person has fullest opportunity to defend himself, while in case of preventive detention, the opportunity that he has for contesting the action of the Executive is very limited. Therefore, the "restrictions placed on a person preventively detained must, consistently with the effectiveness of detention, be minimal".

In *Hussainara Khatoon v. Home Secretary, State of Bihar* [cxcvi] While dealing with the provision of Sub-section (5) of Section 167 of the Code, the Supreme Court has emphasised that if in any case triable by a Magistrate as a summons case the investigation is not concluded within a period of 6 months from the date on which the accused was arrested the Magistrate must make an order stopping further investigation into the offence, unless the officer making the investigation satisfies the Magistrate for Special reasons and in the interest of justice, the continuation of the investigation beyond the period of 6 months is necessary. It was emphasised therein that the provision of said Sub-section (5) of Section 167 of the Code should be strictly complied with.

In *Jayendra Vishnu Thakur Vs. State of Maharashtra* [cxcvii] the court had proceeded on the basis that the right of confrontation is not a fundamental right or whereby accused's fundamental right has not been breached. Article 21, however, envisages a fair trial ; a fair procedure and a fair investigation. By reason of such a right alone the appellant was entitled not only to be informed about his fundamental right and statutory rights but it was obligatory on the part of the Special Public Prosecutor to place on record of the requisite materials before the learned Designated Judge.

In *Prem Shankar Shukla Vs. Delhi Administration* [cxcviii] the court held that ,the guarantee of human dignity forms part of an Constitutional culture and the positive provisions of Articles 14, 19 and 21 spring into action to disshackle any man since to manacle man is more than to mortify him; it is to dehumanize him and, therefore, to violate his very personhood, too often using the mask of 'dangerousness' and security. Even a prisoner is a person not an animal, and an under-trial prisoner is a fortiori so. Our nations founding document admits of no exception. Therefore, all measures authorised by the law must be taken by the Court to keep the stream of prison justice unsullied.

In *Rama Murthy vs. State of Karnataka* [cxcix] this petition has its origin in a letter from one Rama Murthy, a prisoner in Central Jail. Bangalore, addressed to the Hon'ble Chief Justice of this Court. In the letter the main grievance was about denial of rightful wages to the prisoners despite doing hardwork by them in different sections of the prison. Mention was also made about "non-eatable food" and "mental and physical torture". On the matter being taken up judicially, a need was felt, in view of the denial of the allegations in the objection filed on behalf of the respondent, that the District Judge, Bangalore, should visit the Central Jail and should find out the pattern of payment of wages and also the general conditions of the prisoners such as residence, sanitation, food, medicine etc. recapitulate the directions we have given on the way to various authorities. These are:

(1) To take appropriate decision on the recommendations of the Law Commission of India made in its 78th Report on the subject of 'Congestion of undertrial prisoners in jail' as contained in Chapter 9, (Para 20A).

(2) To apply mind to the suggestions of the Mulla Committee as contained in Chapter 20 of Volume I of its Report relating to streamlining the remission system and premature release (parole), and then to do the needful). (Para 23).

(3) To consider the question of entrusting the duty of producing UTPs on remand dates to the prison staff.(Para P7).

(4) To deliberate about enacting of new Prison Act to replace century old Indian Prison Act, 1894'. (Para31).

(5) To examine the question of framing of a model new All India Jail Manual as indicated in para 31.

(6) To reflect on the recommendations of Mulla Committee made in Chapter 29 on the subject of giving proper medical facilities and maintaining appropriate hygienic conditions and to take needed steps.(Paras 35 and 36).

(7) To ponder about the need of complaint box in all the jails. (Para 37).

(8)To think about introduction of liberalisation of communication facilities. (Para 40).

(9)To take needful steps for streamlining of jail visits as indicated in para 42.

(10)To ruminate on the question of introduction of open air prisons at least in the District Headquarters of
the country. (Para 48).

The court have also commented that and our prisons should reform houses as well, in which case the social and economic costs of incarceration would become moreworth while. There seems to be no cause for disillusionment, despite what has been stated in this regard by Roy D. King and Rod Morgan in 'The Future of Prison System'. According to us, talk about treatment and training in prisons is not rhetoric; it can prove, to be real, given the zeal and determination. And we
cannot afford to fail in this sphere as a sound prison system is a crying need of our time in the backdrop of great increase in the numbers of prisoners and that top of various types and from different strata of society.Court have stressed upon improving our prison system by introducing new techniques of management and by educating the prison staff with our constitutional obligations towards prisoners.

In *Prem Shankar v. Delhi Administration* [cc];State of Bihar was prohibited for putting of undertrial prisoners in leg-irons.

In *Sheela Barse v. Union Territory*[cci] Supreme Court was called upon to decide as to when an insane person can be detained in a prison. In Sheela Barse case it was held that jailing of non-criminal mentally ill persons is unconstitutional and directions were given to stop confinement of such persons.It would be of some interest to point that in Sheela Barse, an order was passed to acquaint the ChiefSecretaries of every State with the decision and he was directed to furnish some information to theStanding Counsel of his State.

In *Common Cause v. Union of India*[ccii] "Common Cause", a registered society espousing public causes has asked for certain general directions in this writ petition, under Article 32 of the Constitution of India, with respect to cases pending in criminal courts all over the country. The directions asked for are:quashing of all proceedings against persons accused of offences under the Motor Vehicles Act where the proceedings were initiated more than one year ago and are still pending in any court in the country; and to direct the unconditional release of the accused and dismissal of all proceedings pending in Criminal Courts with respect to offences under Indian Penal Code or other penal statutes which have been pending for more than three years from the date of their institution and for which offences the maximum sentence provided under law is not more than six months - with or without fine. This direction is sought in respect of all prosecutions whether lodged by police, other governmental agency or by a private complainant;

Court gave of the opinion that it is a matter of common experience that in many cases where the persons are accused of minor offences punishable not more than three years - or even less - with or without fine, the proceedings are kept pending for years together. If they are poor and helpless, they languish in jails for long periods either because there is no one to bail them out or because there is no one to think of them. The very pendency of criminal proceedings for long periods by itself operates as an engine of oppression. Quite often, the private complainants institute these proceedings out of oblique motives. Even in case of offences punishable for seven years or less - with or without fine - the prosecutions are kept pending for years and years together in criminal courts. In a majority of these cases, whether instituted by police or private complainants, the accused belong to poorer sections of the society, who are unable to afford competent legal advice. Instances have also come before courts where the accused, who are in jail, are not brought to the court on every date of hearing and for that reason also the cases undergo several adjournments. It appears essential to issue appropriate directions to protect and effectuate the right to life and liberty of the citizens guaranteed by Article 21 of the Constitution. The court stressed on the necessary to ensure that these criminal prosecutions do not operate as engines of oppression and gave directions in this regard to the State governments.

Conclusion

Most of the prisons In India suffer from overcrowding and human rights violations are happening there. Even the cases of homosexuality, tuberculosis and taking of drugs are becoming common news in prisons. Although in the light of the decisions and directions given by the court the condition has improved to a great extent. Prisons are the places where the prisoners suffer the punishment but they are also places of reform. The concept of open jail is also getting popular. The prisoners are trained and engaged in various trades so that they can earn their livelihood. Recently "jail-waani" radio channel has been started to motivate the creativity in the prisoners. There is a need to carry out the reforms in the criminal justice system so that the overcrowding in the prisons should be controlled and they should be prevented from various diseases and tortures caused due to that. Prisons should be managed as per the human right norms and should become a better place for the inmates.

Essay-XII

ROLE OF NGOs as HUMAN RIGHTS DEFENDERS

The spectrum of functions of NGOs as human rights defenders is very wide, ranging from legal awareness to governmental participation on the one hand to social movements to human rights advocacy on the other hand. In the contemporary Indian society, justice is not easily accessible to everyone. Majority of people are either illiterate or semi-literate, most of the strata is ignorant in terms of legal education. Men or women, tribal or minorities, laborers or consumers or the common inhabitants all need some kind of support network when their rights are at stake. Various NGOs have been working in India advocating on the issues of common masses related to human rights consisting of the right to life and its related ingredients like health, education, living, environment etc.

Overview of the concept of NGOs.
The term NGO is broad and ambiguous. It covers a range of organizations within civil society, from political action groups to sports clubs. Its clear definition still remains contested. However, it can be argued that all NGO's can be regarded as civil society organizations though not all civil society organizations are NGO's. The concept of NGO came into use in 1945 following the establishment of the United Nations Organizations which recognized the need to give a consultative role to organizations which were not classified as government nor member states (Willett, 2002). The roots of NGOs are different according to the geographical and historical context. They have recently been regarded as part of the "third sector" or not-for-profit organizations. Although there is contestation of the definition of an

NGO, it is widely accepted that these are organizations which pursue activities to relieve the suffering, promote interests of the poor, protect the environment, provide basic social services, and undertake community development (Cleary, 1997). The majority of these organizations is charity organizations, and thus would not fall under the category of development-oriented NGOs. In this document the term NGO is primarily used for organizations other than charitable organizations.

Relations between NGOs, the State and the People.
There is no doubt that with increasing demands on the state by the citizens, the state can no longer be the sole provider of goods and services. It is also true that the support and interest in NGOs has grown as a result of the failure by state agencies to deliver services. Thus, the state and NGOs need each other. In terms of their relation with the state, Clark (1991) provides a liberalist view in terms of three options; they can complement, reform, and/or oppose the state.

In their role of complementing the state, they act as the implementers of development activities. In this case as argued by Thomas, (1992) NGOs fill the gaps left by the public service. The role of the state becomes more of an enabler rather than a provider of services. In their reforming role NGOs are seen as agents of advocacy and contribute immensely to policy dialogue. NGOs are able to represent the interests of the people they work with and in this case can ensure that policies are adaptable to real life situations. Finally, NGOs can oppose the state. They can do this by acting as watchdogs and holding the state accountable. This can be achieved through several methods including lobbying or even overtly supporting groups which are adversely affected by the policies of the government.

They contribute to standard setting as well as to the promotion, implementation and enforcement of human rights norms. They provoke and energies. They spread the massage of human rights and mobilize people to realize that massage. Decentralized and diverse, they proceed with speed, decisiveness and range of concerns impossible to imagine in relation to most of the work of executive and political constrained intergovernmental organizations. NGOs operate on the basis of differing mandates, each responding to its own priorities and methods of action, bringing a range of viewpoints of the human rights movement.

Within individual states, it is often the domestic human rights NGOs that call governments to account and compel reconsideration of politics and programs that have been designed its disregard or violation of human rights norms. It is not only domestic policies of a state that figure in NGOs reporting and advocacy. The development in few states of a foreign economic policy that takes into account human rights violation in other states owes much to information provided and pressures exerted by NGOs. NGOs are effectively performing the work of representation of the voiceless and to help vocalize the interests of persons not well-represented in policymaking; Service provision. NGOs can deliver technical expertise on particular topics as needed by government officials as well as participate directly in operational activities; Monitoring and assessment. NGOs can help strengthen international agreements by monitoring negotiation efforts and governmental compliance ad in legitimization of global-scale decision making mechanisms. NGOs are broadening the base of information for decision making, improving the quality, authoritativeness, and legitimacy of the policy choices of international organizations.

Human rights movements were common in India in the name of voluntarism which has a long history. During the freedom struggle these movements received an impetus from the work of religious and social reformers and national leaders, notably Raja Ram Mohan Roy, Swami Dayananda, Swami Ramakrishna, Vivekananda, Anni Besant and Mahatma Gandhi. All these social movements were actually aimed at the protection, promotion and preservation of the human rights of marginalized people. Such earliest of social movements in India could be traced to the Gandhian efforts of Sarvodaya. Since 1970s a number of social movements emphasizing on a range of basic human rights issues have come to animate the sphere of civil society.

In recent times, many grassroots micro movements also known as new social movements have been taking place centering on contemporary issues of importance such as ecology, environment, women empowerment, human rights, sharing of natural resources and the like. The NGOs in India have contributed handsomely towards human rights activism through intense campaigns, people's mobilization programmes and effective networks.

Different Human Rights Movements run by NGOs in India
CHIPKO MOVEMENT

The Chipko movement or Chipko Andolan (literally "to stick" in Hindi) is a social ecological movement that practiced the Gandhian methods of satyagrah and non-violent resistance, through the act of hugging trees to protect them from falling. This movement is led by Sundarlal Bahuguna. The modern Chipko movement started in the early 1970s in the Garhwal Himalayas of Uttarakhand, with growing awareness towards rapid deforestation. The landmark event in this struggle took place on March 26, 1974, when a group of peasant women in Reni village, Hemwalghati, in Chamoli district, Uttarakhand, India, acted to prevent the cutting of trees and reclaim their traditional forest rights that were threatened by the contractor system of the state Forest Department. Their actions inspired hundreds of such actions at the grassroots level throughout the region. By the 1980s the movement had spread throughout India and led to formulation of people-sensitive forest policies, which put a stop to the open felling of trees in regions as far reaching as Vindhyas and the Western Ghats.

The Chipko movement though primarily a livelihood movement rather than a forest conservation movement went on to become a rallying point for many future environmentalists, environmental protests and movements the world over and created a precedent for non-violent protest. The slogan of Chipko movement is 'ecology is economy'. It occurred at a time when there was hardly any environmental movement in the developing world, and its success meant that the world immediately took notice of this non-violent Tree hugging movement, which was to inspire in time many such eco-groups by helping to slow down the rapid deforestation, expose vested interests, increase ecological awareness, and demonstrate the viability of people power.

THE APPIKO MOVEMENT

The Appiko movement was a revolutionary movement based on environmental conservation in India. The Chipko movement (Hug the Trees Movement) in Uttarakhand in the Himalayas inspired the villagers of the district of Karnataka province in southern India to launch a similar movement to save their forests. In September 1983, movement was led by Panduranga Hegde along with the men, women and children of Salkani "hugged the trees" in Kalase forest. (The local term for "hugging" in Kannada is appiko.) Appiko movement gave birth to a new awareness all over southern India.

In 1950, Uttarakhand district forest covered more than 81 percent of its geographical area. The government, declaring this forest district a "backward" area, then initiated the process of "development". Their major industries - a pulp and paper mill, a plywood factory and a chain of hydroelectric dams constructed to harness the rivers - sprouted in the area. These industries have overexploited the forest resource, and the dams have submerged huge-forest and agricultural areas. The forest had shrunk to nearly 25 percent of the district's area by 1980. The local populations, especially the poorest groups were displaced by the dams. The conversion of the natural mixed forests into teak and eucalyptus plantations dried up the water sources, directly affecting forest dwellers. In a nutshell, the three major p's - paper, plywood and power - which were intended for the development of the people, have resulted in a fourth p: poverty.

NARMADA BACHAO AANDOLAN

Narmada Bachao Andolan is the most powerful mass movement, started in 1985, against the construction of huge dam on the Narmada River. Narmada is the India's largest west flowing river, which supports a large variety of people with distinguished culture and tradition ranging from the indigenous (tribal) people inhabited in the jungles here to the large number of rural population. The proposed Sardar Sarovar Dam and Narmada Sagar will displace more than 250,000 people. The big fight is over the resettlement or the rehabilitation of these people. The two proposals are already under construction, supported by US$550 million loan by the World Bank. There are plans to build over 3000 big and small dams along the river.

Led by one of the prominent leader Medha Patkar, it has now been turned into the International protest, gaining support from NGOs all around the globe. Protestors are agitating the issue through the mass media, hunger strikes, massive marches, rallies and the through the on screen of several documentary films. Although they have been protesting peacefully, but they been harassed, arrested and beaten up by the police several times. The Narmada Bachao Andolan has been pressurizing the World Bank to withdraw its loan from the project through media.

THE DALIT ANDOLAN

One of the problems of the Left in India has been its inability to combine caste with class into an inclusive political agenda. From other political formations has come, at best, compassion and sympathy, including as mentioned earlier from Gandhi, but not political empowerment that could lead to political rights. The two most influential thinkers and leaders to that end have come from within the dalits, namely Jyotirao Phule and B.R.Ambedkar.

The dalit social and cultural movements have remained robust and active within the civil society, drawing their strength from Phule and Ambedkar. But like the Left movements, different strains have come up, often not in harmony with each other. They received international notice for their fierce protests at the International Conference on Racism in Durban some years back when the Indian Government refused to have the issue of Dalits included in the Conference agenda. They form an important component of the upcoming World Social Forum in Mumbai in January 2004.

JHOLA ANDOLAN

Jhola Aandolan is a mass movement of Paryawaran Sachetak Samiti to promote eco-friendly carry bags and make a polythene-free world. The campaign started since April 22, 1999 (International Earth Day). Paryawaran Sachetak Samiti conducts those activities which demonstrate community based approaches that not only reduce the rate of global warming, but also create awareness to develop a healthy climate in the entire target population through information, education and communication training component in order to develop a eco-friendly atmosphere for the entire world. Jhola Aandolan events work on the "IEC" (Information, Education and Communication) principle. In 2001 a memorandum was submitted to the Prime Minister of India with 100,000 signatures of individual citizens of India through public participation.

SWADHYAY MOVEMENT

Swadhyay movement is movement of self-transformation and self-empowerment, started by Pandurang Vaijanath Athavale. This movement works for social improvement of lower caste, collective farming, protection of trees and water conservation as well as harvesting. Swadhyay movement is primarily based on Reverence to the Earth, Reverence to the Mother Nature.

GAY RIGHTS MOVEMENT

The Gay Rights Movement is also known as the Lesbian, gay and transgender rights movement and it is a movement for the protection of sexual interests of the gays and lesbians. The transgender or homosexual activities were always termed as illegal and asocial in the society and homosexual people were often thrown out of the society as outcasts. Prior to the early 20th century, the gays and lesbians were declared as criminals and they were treated under the laws of sodomy and sumptuary. However, the dawn of the 20th Century brought a new ray of hope in the lives of gays and lesbians.

Gay Rights: Position in India

The British obviously found the practice unchristian and abhorrent and in 1860, enacted the Indian Penal Code which in Section 377 states: "Unnatural offenses - Whoever voluntarily has carnal intercourse against the order of nature with any man, woman, animal shall be punished with imprisonment for life, or with imprisonment of either description for a term which may extend to 10 years, and shall be liable to fine. Consent of the other party is completely irrelevant for conviction, but it may be a relevant consideration while fixing the quantum of punishment. It must be pointed out that homosexuality per se is not an offense and an "act" of unnatural intercourse has to be proved.

In India, in the previous century, legislatures and judiciaries across the globe have upheld laws criminalizing homosexuality and transgender behaviour, justifying them on grounds of public decency and morality. With the advent of the contemporary epoch, the movement against the repressive and oppressive nature of Section 377 grew exponentially and reached its culmination in *Naz Foundation v. Government of NCT of Delhi*, wherein the Delhi High Court recognized the anachronism associated with Section 377 and interpreted it to exclude sexual acts between consenting adults, thus decriminalizing homosexuality. Although the ramifications are limited and may be quelled by an act of Parliament, the judgment is a landmark in civil liberties litigation and may be regarded as one of the stepping stones to the emancipation of the sexual minorities in India from tyranny and coercion at the hands of the law.

SAVE SILENT VALLEY

Save Silent Valley was a social movement aimed at the protection of Silent valley, an evergreen tropical forest in the Palakkad district of Kerala, India. It was started in 1973 to save the Silent Valley Reserve Forest in from being flooded by a hydroelectric project. The valley was declared as Silent Valley National Park in 1985. Kerala Sasthra Sahithya Parishath (KSSP) effectively aroused public opinion on the requirement to save Silent Valley. They also published a Techno-economic and Socio-Political assessment report on the Silent Valley Hydroelectric project. The Kerala Sastra Sahitya Parishad (KSSP) has earned international recognition in 1995 for its work in mobilising public opinion among people's organizations in the State of Kerala. The KSSP is regarded as one of the best-informed and best-organized grassroots movement in India, with over 20000 members. The poet activist Sugathakumari played an important role in the silent valley protest and her poem "Marathinu Stuthi" (Ode to a Tree) became a symbol for the protest from the intellectual community and was the opening song/prayer of most of the "save the Silent Valley" campaign meetings.

PEASANTRY MOVEMENTS

Shetkari Sanghatana - Farmers' Organisation in Maharashtra, led by Sharad Joshi, articulate spokesman of the new farmer's movement. Agriculturist and Peasant Leader and at national level, of the Kisan Coordination Committee (KCC) comprising of sister organisations from 14 states - Maharashtra, Karnataka, Gujarat, Rajasthan, Punjab, Haryana, Himachal Pradesh, Madhya Pradesh, Bihar, Uttar Pradesh, Orissa, Andhra Pradesh, Tamil Nadu, Kerala; led a number of agitations in Maharashtra, Karnataka, Gujarat , Punjab, Haryana etc. for remunerative prices of onions, sugar cane, tobacco, milk, paddy, cotton, against hike in electricity tariffs, for liquidation of rural debts and against State dumping in domestic markets.

Karnataka Rajya Rayot Sangha, also known as KRRS or the Karnataka Rajya Raitha Sangha, is a farmer's movement. M. D. Nanjundaswamy was the president of the organisation. It came to lime light for its opposition to KFC shops in Bangalore in the 1990s. They are in the forefront of fighting multinational companies that try to sell terminator seeds, like Monsanto Company.

SULABH INTERNATIONAL SOCIAL SERVICE ORGANISATION

In 1970, Dr. Bindeshwar Pathak founded a non-profit making voluntary social organisation, Sulabh Shauchalaya Sansthan, (now known as Sulabh International Social Service Organisation) to carry out the work of liberation of scavengers from the sub-human practice of manual excreta cleaning in India and other related jobs. In 1984, the first Sulabh public toilet linked biogas plant was set up at Adalatganj, Patna. It produced electricity from biogas which was supplied to the 3 kms long Bailey Road, Patna. In 2005, Sulabh International Academy of Environmental Sanitation registered under the Societies Registration Act 1860 by the Registrar, Registration, Govt of Delhi. 23 professionals from 5 countries attended the "International Workshop on Sanitation Technologies" organized by Sulabh International Academy of Environmental Sanitation in collaboration with UN – Habitat and UNDP. Sulabh organized the World Toilet Summit 2007 in collaboration with WTO.

JOAR (JHARKHAND ORGANISATION AGAINST RADIATION)

Jharkhand Organisation against Radiation is a Social Movement running from last 20 years for the awareness of masses about ill-effect of radioactive radiation caused by Uranium Corporation of India and also struggling for inhuman practices like without any treatment hazardous waste are discharged in nearby ponds by the Uranium Corporation of India which led to serious environmental problem and health problem even disabilities by birth. JOAR is started by Ghanshyam Biruli in Jadugudda and Bhatin district of Jharkhand. Professor H. Koide (Kyoto University) and Dr. Sanghamitra Gadekar (editor Anumukti) had studied about the adverse effect on the health of indigenous people.

JAN LOKPAL BILL MOVEMENT

Another major social movement has been that of Anna Hazare who has been fighting since more than two decades for bringing about transparency in bureaucratic apparatus of the state. His movement has changed his village Ralegon Siddhi in Maharashtra into a model village. His movement emphasises the right of the common people to know the information regarding government initiatives and the implementation procedures of the welfare schemes. His effort made the "Right to Information Act" a reality. The government is being pressurized to enact the "JAN-LOKPAL" Act. This legislation would entail the right of the people to gain remedy against government officials' malpractices and thereby bring transparency and accountability in the functioning of the government. This would ultimately serve to check corruption and rent-seeking practices.

HUMAN RIGHTS ADVOCACY

Though the judiciary was conceived as an arm of social revolution, its contribution towards human rights protection remained insignificant until the development of Public Interest Litigation. Lawyers and Judges concentrated their attention to their day to day work and are not ale to fulfill the demands of justice.The common rule of *locus standi* is relaxed so as to enable the Court to look into the grievances complained on behalf of the poor, the depraved, the illiterate and the disabled who cannot vindicate the legal wrong or legal injury caused to them for any violation of any constitutional or legal right. [cciii]When the Court is prima facie satisfied about variation of any constitutional right of a group of people belonging to the disadvantaged category, it may not allow the State or the Government from raising the question as to the maintainability of the petition.

In a Public Interest Litigation, filed by an NGO, *Centre for Enquiry into Health and Allied Themes (CEHAT) and others Vs. Union of India and others*, Supreme Court has issued directions on 4th May 2001 to the Central Government, State Governments and appropriate authorities to take steps for effective implementation of law for preventing female infanticide with thwe help if he Medical Council of India.

Supreme Court in *Rural Litigation and Entitlement Kendra v. State of U. P.* stated very clearly and firmly set about finding the golden harmony between development and environment. It shows that the environmental disasters subsequent to 'the Silent Valley case have jolted and shocked the judicial consciousness into realizing that in a State where the citizenry is ignorant, poverty stricken and, the only solution to the problem lies in its hands of government. In the present case the issue involved was the mining of lime stones in the *'Doon Valley'* which threatened to destroy the flora, fauna and populace of that region. The prompt action of the Supreme Court was to stop the mining operations carried out through blasting was needed.

In another case *BALCO Employees' Union (Regd.) v. Union of India*[cciv], it was held ,"While PIL initially was invoked mostly in cases connected with the relief to the people and the weaker sections of the society and in areas where there was violation of human rights under Article 21, but with the passage of time, petitions have been entertained in other spheres."

Bandhua Mukti Morcha v. Union of India [ccv] PIL was filed complaining that inspite of Article 23 of the Constitution and the Bonded Labours System (Abolition) Act, 1976, the practice was prevalent in stone quarries in Faridabad District where a large number of labourers from Maharashtra, Madhya Pradesh, Uttar Pradesh and Rajasthan were working as bonded labourers under inhuman and intolerable conditions. This matter shocked the conscience of the Bench hearing the matter and the human rights of the bonded laborers were protected.

Employment of child labour again received attention of the Supreme Court in Labourers working in *Salal Hydro Project Vs. State of J.& K.*[ccvi]and the Court, once again, following its decision in Asian Games case held that no child below the age of 14 years could be employed as it violated the constitutional mandate of Art.24.

The case of *Rural Litigation and Entitlement Kendra v. State of U.P.*[ccvii],brings into sharp focus the conflict between development and conservation and emphasizes the need for reconciling the two in the in *People's Union For Democratic Rights v. State of Bihar*[ccviii] only shows that the Court is not prepared to give up this new remedy developed by it through public interest litigation to compensate the victims. The petitioner, an NGO committed to upholding of fundamental rights of citizens, had moved the court under Article 32 of the Constitution alleging that the police opened fire as a result of which several received injuries and at least 21 died. The Court, therefore, directed that without prejudice to the just claim for compensation.

In the case of *Joint Women's Programme v. State of Bihar*, also re-enforces this conclusion. The Court in this case, was informed of two dowry deaths and slackness in investigation thereof. The Court directed the two State Governments to create sub-jury cells at the State level to investigate dowry-deaths through a specialized investigative units. In *Bihar Legal Support Society v. Chief Justice of India*, the Court was told that it was not proper to attach urgency or importance to the case of an industrialist, The Court took this opportunity to reassure that in fact this court has always regarded the poor and the disadvantageous as entitled to preferential consideration than the rich and the affluent, the businessmen and the industrialists. The Court, therefore, dispelled the doubt that it was not giving to the "small men" the same treatment as it is giving to the "big industrialists".

The judgment in the case of *Vishakha Vs. State of Rajasthan*[xcix] contains a specific direction that the guidelines and norms set out therein would be strictly observed at all work places for the preservation and enforcement of a right to gender equality of all working women. A women who was working as a social worker was gang raped by the group of villagers, an NGO named *Vishakha* fought for her cause. The Supreme Court has held that its directions would be binding and enforceable in law until suitable legislation is enacted to occupy the field. The right to gender equality is intrinsic to the right to life under Article 21 of the Constitution. The right to life comprehends the right to live with dignity.

The Supreme Court noted that there was a global acceptance by International Conventions of the common minimum requirements of this right. The Convention on the Elimination of All Forms of Discrimination against Women (CEDAW) requires all States who are parties thereto to take appropriate measures to eliminate discrimination against women in the field of employment in order to ensure, on a basis of equality of men and women, the same rights, in particular. The right to work as an inalienable right of all human beings; and the right to protection of health and safety in working conditions.

Conclusion

Many a times it is found that the NGOs behave just like a catalyst in the society which simply quickens the process of change and development. Sometimes it can be observed that the social revolution in itself contain all the virtues of an NGO. NGOs behave as the protectors of the core rights and patrons for legal renaissance in the form of social movements resulting into changes in legal norms in the society. NGOs have emancipated and developed new laws and even legislative directions have taken their turn by way of amending, changing and deletion of the existing laws which are not needed in the particular time being in force. There is, therefore, a need to empower NGOs with the ability to source funds and help them realize their goals. Insufficient funding would be facilitated by granting NGOs access to alternative financial resources, such as government and supporters. Alternative sources of funding will assist particularly small NGOs. Training and development in areas of organizational, project and financial and legal management, as well as capacity building represent some of the measures which are needed in order to improve NGOs participation in promoting justice to the marginalized people. Equipping NGOs with legal skills by interconnecting them with the bar, bench and law schools would allow them to effectively lobby government would also help NGOs effectively campaign for justice.

The establishment of partnerships with local, regional, and international institutions would improve the management of NGOs by providing lessons learnt from the experiences and successes of a number of different multinational non-governmental organizations.

BIBLIOGRAPHY:

BOOKS:

A.K JHA, CHILD ABUSE AND HUMAN RIGHTS, IST EDITION, PUBLICATION 2000

Anne Aranny, Francis,Wandy Waring, Pam Stavropouls Joan Kirkby. Gender Studies Terms And Debates, Palgrave Macmillan Publishers, 1st Edition 2003.

Bare Act of Information Technology Act, 2000, Universal Publication

Child Marriages and the Law in India, Human Rights Law Network, June 2005.

Confronting Cyber-bullying by Shaheen Shariff

Coomaraswamy, Radhika (2005), 'Human Security and Gender Violence', Economic and Political Weekly, October 29

Cyber Crime and the Victimization of Women **By:** Debarati Halder; K. Jaishankar

Cyber Crimes And Fraud Management, Indian Institute of Banking & Finance

Cyber laws by Justice Yatinder Singh, 4th edition

Cyber security operations handbook by John W. Ritting and William m.

Hancock

Cyber sexualities, a reader on feminist theory, cyborgs and cyberspace edited by Jenny Wolmark

Dorothy Q. Thomas, Domestic Violence as a Human Rights Issue, Human Rights Quarterly, Vol. 15, No. 1 (Feb., 1993)

Gender And Discrimination- Role Of Women In India- Oxford University Press 2011

Indira Jaisant – Handbook On Law Of Domestic Violence, 1st Edition 2009 Lexis Nexis, New Delhi

Jain, M.P. Indian Constitutional Law, Sixth Edition, Nagpur: Lexis Nexis Butterworths Wadhwa, 2012.

K Uma Devi, Women in Unorganised Sector: quest for Social Justice, [2010] Regal Publications, New Delhi

Kathy Davis, Mary Evans, Judith Lorber, Handbook Of Gender And Women's Studies, Sage Publications, 2006 Edition.

Laya Medhini et al, HIV/AIDS AND THE LAW (New Delhi: Human Rights Law Network, 2007)

M. Shenoy – Domestic Violence Issues And Perspctives,1st Edition 2007, Aavishkar Publications, Jaipur

M.P.Jain, *Indian Constitutional Law*, [6th Edn,2011], Lexis Nexis, Nagpur

Meerambika Mahapatro ,The risk factor of domestic violence in India; Indian Journal of Community Medicine, 2012 Vol.37 Issue 3

Michael S. Kimmel, The Gendered Society, Oxford University Press, 2nd Edition 2004

Mishra S.N., Indian Penal Code

Neha Arora, Human Rights And Gender Voilance, RBSA Publishers Jaipur, 1st Edition 2012.

Om Gupta, Media Society and Culture, [2006] Isha Books New Delhi

Padmalaya Mahapatra, Domestic violence: issue of violation of human rights of women, Madhya Pradesh Journal of Social Sciences 2008

Pandey, J.N. Constitution of India, Allahabad: Central Law Agency, 50th Edition.

Pooja Juyal, Women's Studies in India: Some Contemporary Contours, 2005 Ewha Women University Press, South Korea

Prostitution and Beyond: An Analysis of Sex Work in India (New Delhi: SAGE Publishers, 2008)

Radhika Coomaraswamy, Men's Laws Women's Lives, a Constitutional Perspective on Religion, Common law and culture in South Asia. Indira Jaising ed. New Delhi, 2005.

Raj Bahadur Singh Verma, Towards Empowering Indian Women: Mapping Specifics of Tasks in Crucial Sectors, 2007 Serials Publications, New Delhi

Ratanlal & Dhirajlal, The Indian Penal Code, Lexis Nexis Butterworths Wadhwa, Nagpur, 33 Edition, 2010

Ratanlal & Dhirajlal, The Law Of Evidence, Wadhwa Publications, Nagpur, 1985

S.K PACHAURI, CHILDREN AND HUMAN RIGHTS, 1999 PUBLICATION

S.P SHAW, ENCYCLOPAEDIA OF LAWS OF THE CHILD IN INDIA, 1st EDITION 2000

Sally Engle Merry- Human Rights : Gender Violence- Transalating International Law Into Local Justice- Oxford University Press, India 2009

Sanchari Roy Mukherjee, Indian women: broken words, distant dreams, 2007 Levant Books, Kolkata

Satya P Kanan, Encyclopedia Of Human Rights And Social Justice, Dominant Publishers, 1st Edition 2006.

Seervai H M, Constitutional Law Of India, 4th Edition, Silver Jubilee Edition, Volume 2, Universal Law Publishing co. Pvt. Ltd.

Social Status Of Women In India- Maya Majumdar – Wisdom Press THE HINDU

V.N.Shukla, Constitutional Law of India, 7th edition, Allahabad Law Agency, 2012

VN Shukla, *Constitutional Law of India*, [11th edn., 2008] Eastern Book Company, Lucknow

Women And Human Rights – Anju Bindra- Manglam Publishers Delhi 2007

Women And The Rule Of Law- Sumanlata- Akansha Publishing House

Women In Distress- Neela Dabir- Rawat Publications

Women Work And Family – H.L Kalia- Rawat Publications

ARTICLES

Being Female Can Be Fatal: An Examination Of India's Ban On Pre-Natal Gender Testing- Andrea Krugman- Cardozo J. Of Int'l & Comp. Law- [Vol. 6:215] 1998

UN Women, "Definition of forced and child marriage "http://www.endvawnow.org/en/articles/614-definition-of-forced-and-child-marriage.html

Family Planning Policies And Resultant Discrimination Against The Girl Child -A Study Of India And China -Anjana Agarwal- Singapore Law Review (2009) 27 Sing.L.Rev. 161-178

33(10) ECONOMIC AND POLITICAL WEEKLY 504 (1998)

Female Feticide In India-Nehaluddin Ahmad- Issues In Law & Medicine, Volume 26, Number 1, 2010

Son Preference In India: Implications For Gender Development. Aparna

Mitra. Department of Economics.University of Oklahom.

AIPWA: On *Sexual Harassment* at *Workplace* Available on http://aipwa-aipwa.blogspot.in/2012/12/0n-sexual-harassment-at-workplace-this.html

Alicia Ely Yamin, Defining Questions: Situating Issues of Power in the Formulation of a Right to Health underInternational Law, Human Rights Quarterly, Vol. 18, No. 2 (May, 1996), pp. 398-438

Alicia Ely Yamin, Defining Questions: Situating Issues of Power in the Formulation of a Right to Health underInternational Law, Human Rights Quarterly, Vol. 18, No. 2 (May, 1996), pp. 398-438

Anil Awachat, *Prostitution in Pune and Bombay: A Report*, 21 (12) ECONOMIC AND POLITICAL WEEKLY 478 (1986)

CNN – IBN (5 september 2012) 'India moves to protect women from sexual harassment at work'Available on ininlive.in.com>ibnlive>India

DIXON-MUELLER, POPULATION PouCIES AND WOMEN'S RIGHTS: TRANSFORMING REPRODUCTIVE CHOICE 12 (1993)

DIXON-MUELLER, POPULATION PouCIES AND WOMEN'S RIGHTS: TRANSFORMING REPRODUCTIVE CHOICE 12 (1993)

Does India Still Need Khap Panchayats? By pamposh raina on Hindustan times October 23, 2012

Donald Light, Comparative Models of "Health Care" Systems, in THE SOCIOLOGY OF HEALTH AND ILLNESS, supra note 36, at 457

Donald Light, Comparative Models of "Health Care" Systems, in THE SOCIOLOGY OF HEALTH AND ILLNESS, supra note 36, at 457

Flaws in the Sexual Harassment Of Women Act by Express News Service-BANGLORE published:21st September 2012 9:43 available on newindianexpress.com>Home>karnataka

Frances M. Shaver, *Prostitution: A Critical Analysis of Three Policy Approaches*, 11(3) CANADIAN PUBLIC POLICY 493 (1985)

Geetanjali Gangoli, Prostitution, Legalisation and Decriminalisation: Recent Debates,

H.D.C. ROSCAM ABBING, INTERNATIONAL ORGANIZATIONS IN EUROPE AND THE RIGHT TO HEALTH CARE 104-05 (1979); Roemer, supra note 3, at 17

H.D.C. ROSCAM ABBING, INTERNATIONAL ORGANIZATIONS IN EUROPE AND THE RIGHT TO HEALTH CARE 104-05 (1979); Roemer, supra note 3, at 17

Henry Steiner, Political Participation as a Human Right, 1 HARV. HUM. RTS. Y.B. 77 (1988).

Henry Steiner, Political Participation as a Human Right, 1 HARV. HUM. RTS. Y.B. 77 (1988).

http://www.hindunet.org/hindu_history/sudheer_history/practices1.html

India's New Labour Law- Prevention Of Sexual Harassment At Workplace available on www.mondaq.com/india on 9th May 2013

JACK DONNELLY, UNIVERSAL HUMAN RIGHTS IN THEORY AND PRACTICE (1989)

JACK DONNELLY, UNIVERSAL HUMAN RIGHTS IN THEORY AND PRACTICE (1989)

Janice C. Raymond, *Prostitution on Demand: Legalizing Buyers as Sexual Consumers*, 10(10) VIOLENCE AGAINST WOMEN 1156 (2004)

Jean D' Cunha, Prostitution Laws: Ideological Dimensions and Enforcement Practices, 27(17) ECONOMIC AND POLITICAL WEEKLY WS-34 (1992)

John Knowles, The Responsibility of the Individual, in DOING BETTER AND FEELING WORSE: HEALTH IN THE UNITED STATES (John Knowles ed., 1977)

John Knowles, The Responsibility of the Individual, in DOING BETTER AND FEELING WORSE: HEALTH IN THE UNITED STATES (John

Knowles ed., 1977)

Jonathan Mann et al., Health and Human Rights, 1 HEALTH & HUM. RTs. 6 (1994). 48. See, e.g., WORLD HEALTH ORGANIZATION, DEVELOPMENT OF INDICATORS FOR MONITORING PROGRESS TOWARDS HEALTH FOR ALL BY THE YEAR 2000, at 7 (1981).

Jonathan Mann et al., Health and Human Rights, 1 HEALTH & HUM. RTs. 6 (1994). 48. See, e.g., WORLD HEALTH ORGANIZATION, DEVELOPMENT OF INDICATORS FOR MONITORING PROGRESS TOWARDS HEALTH FOR ALL BY THE YEAR 2000, at 7 (1981).

Joseph M. Boyle, Jr., The Concept of Health and the Right to Health, 3 Soc. THOUGHT, Summer 1977, at 5, 6 (quoting Leon R. Kass, Regarding the End of Medicine and the Pursuit of Health, 40 PUB. INTEREST 39 (1975)

Joseph M. Boyle, Jr., The Concept of Health and the Right to Health, 3 Soc. THOUGHT, Summer 1977, at 5, 6 (quoting Leon R. Kass, Regarding the End of Medicine and the Pursuit of Health, 40 PUB. INTEREST 39 (1975)

Khap panchayat blames dowry, crimes against women for female foeticide by deepender deswal on the times of india. Feb 20, 2013,

Khap Panchayat Tries to Set 'Witch' on Fire in Rajasthan by THE CRONICALS ON January 15, 2013

Laurie Wiseberg, The Opening of A Dialogue, 1 HEALTH & HUM. RTS. 121-24 (1995).

Arora Neha; Human Rights and Gender Violence.

Laurie Wiseberg, The Opening of A Dialogue, 1 HEALTH & HUM. RTS. 121-24 (1995).

Lawrence Gostin & Jonathan Mann, Towards the Development of a Human Rights Impact Assessment for the Formulation and Evaluation of Health Policies, 1 HEALTH & Hum. RTs. 58 (1994

Lawrence Gostin & Jonathan Mann, Towards the Development of a Human Rights Impact Assessment for the Formulation and Evaluation of Health Policies, 1 HEALTH & Hum. RTs. 58 (1994

Lynn Freedman, Reflections on Emerging Frameworks of Health and Human Rights, 1 HEALTH & HUM. RTS. 314, 333 (1995)

Lynn Freedman, Reflections on Emerging Frameworks of Health and Human Rights, 1 HEALTH & HUM. RTS. 314, 333 (1995)

Mary Moran and others, The new landscape of neglected disease drug development (London School of Economics and Political Science and The Wellcome Trust, 2005).

Mary Moran and others, The new landscape of neglected disease drug development (London School of Economics and Political Science and The Wellcome Trust, 2005).

Mishra Jyotsana; Women and Human Rights.

Nahid Toubia, From Health or Human Rights to Health and Human Rights: Where Do We Go From Here?, 1 HEALTH & HUM. RTS. 136, (1995)

Nahid Toubia, From Health or Human Rights to Health and Human Rights: Where Do We Go From Here?, 1 HEALTH & HUM. RTS. 136, (1995)

Philip Alston, The UN's Human Rights Record: From San Francisco to Vienna and Beyond, 16 HUM. RTS. Q. 375, 384-87 (1994).

Philip Alston, The UN's Human Rights Record: From San Francisco to Vienna and Beyond, 16 HUM. RTS. Q. 375, 384-87 (1994).

Press release, National Advisory Concil, January 10,2011,http://nac.nic.in/press_release/10_january_2011.pdf

R.J. VINCENT, HUMAN RIGHTS AND INTERNATIONAL RELATIONS (1986). For a discussion of the mischaracterization of the implications and requirements of social and economic right

R.J. VINCENT, HUMAN RIGHTS AND INTERNATIONAL RELATIONS (1986). For a discussion of the mischaracterization of the implications and requirements of social and economic right

Rebecca J. Cook, Gender, Health and Human Rights, 1 HEALTH & HUM. RTS. 350, 359 (1995)

Rebecca J. Cook, Gender, Health and Human Rights, 1 HEALTH & HUM. RTS. 350, 359 (1995)

Rebecca J. Cook, International Human Rights and Women's Reproductive Health, 24 STUD. FAM. PLAN. 73, 77 (1993)

Rebecca J. Cook, International Human Rights and Women's Reproductive Health, 24 STUD. FAM. PLAN. 73, 77 (1993)

Reed Boland et al., Honoring Human Rights and Population Policies: From Declaration to Action, in POPULATION POLICIEs RECONSIDERED: HEALTH, EMPOWERMENT AND RIGHTS 89 (

Reed Boland et al., Honoring Human Rights and Population Policies: From Declaration to Action, in POPULATION POLICIEs RECONSIDERED: HEALTH, EMPOWERMENT AND RIGHTS 89 (

Robert Crawford, Individual Responsibility and Health Politics, in THE SOCIOLOGY OF HEALTH AND ILLNESS, supra note 36, at 381, 384

Robert Crawford, Individual Responsibility and Health Politics, in THE SOCIOLOGY OF HEALTH AND ILLNESS, supra note 36, at 381, 384

Ruth Roemer, The Right to Health Care, in THE RIGHT TO HEALTH IN THE AMERICAS 17 (Hernan Fuenzalida-Puelma & Susan Scholle Connor eds., 1989

Ruth Roemer, The Right to Health Care, in THE RIGHT TO HEALTH IN THE AMERICAS 17 (Hernan Fuenzalida-Puelma & Susan Scholle Connor eds., 1989

Sandra L. Decker , Medicare and the Health of Women with Breast Cancer,

The Journal of Human Resources, Vol. 40, No. 4 (Autumn, 2005), pp. 948-968

Sandra L. Decker , Medicare and the Health of Women with Breast Cancer, The Journal of Human Resources, Vol. 40, No. 4 (Autumn, 2005), pp. 948-968

Sexual harassment at workplace: Extending the Debate sun, 2012-09-09 12:28 by Ayesha kidwani, Annubhuti Maurya, and Albeena Shakil. www.pragoti.in/node/4762

Sexual Harassment Of Women At Workplace (Prevention , Prohibition and Redressal),Act 2013.

Sexual harassment of women at workplace bill 2012 passed by Lok sabha available on http://www.lawyerscollective.org

Sharma Alka, Garg Ranjeeta, Mohapatra Samapika; Education and Women Empowerment.

Son Preference, Sex Selection And The Problem Of Missing Women In India2009..Deepankar Basu -University Of Massachusetts – Amherst

Theodor Marmor, WHY ARE SOME PEOPLE HEALTHY AND OTHERS NOT? THE DETERMINANTS OF HEALTH OF POPULATIONS (et al. eds., 1994). ."

Theodor Marmor, WHY ARE SOME PEOPLE HEALTHY AND OTHERS NOT? THE DETERMINANTS OF HEALTH OF POPULATIONS (et al. eds., 1994). ."

UNICEF, "Child protection from violence, exploitation and abuse http://www.unicef.org/protection/57929_58008.html

Virginia A. Leary, Implications of a Right to Health, in HUMAN RIGHTS IN THE TWENTY-FIRST CENTURY 481, 485 (Kathleen E. Mahoney & Paul Mahoney eds., 1993).

Virginia A. Leary, Implications of a Right to Health, in HUMAN RIGHTS IN THE TWENTY-FIRST CENTURY 481, 485 (Kathleen E. Mahoney &

Paul Mahoney eds., 1993).

William J. Mayo, The Right to Health, The North American Review, Vol. 211, No. 771 (Feb., 1920), pp. 194-202

William J. Mayo, The Right to Health, The North American Review, Vol. 211, No. 771 (Feb., 1920), pp. 194-202

ACTS REFFERED

Code of Criminal Procedure, 1973

Employers Liabilities Act 1938

Indian Penal Code, 1860.

Juvenile Justice Act, 2000

Mental Health Act, 1987

National Commission for Women Act, 1990 (20 of 1990)

Protection of Women from Domestic Violence Act, 2005

Protection of Women from Domestic Violence act, 2005.

The Beedi & Cigar Workers (Conditions of Employment) Act, 1966

The Bonded Labour System (Abolition) Act, 1979

The Child Labour (Prohibition & Regulation) Act

The Child Marriage Restraint Act, 1929 (19 of 1929)

The Cinematograph Act, 1952

The Commission of Sati (Prevention) Act, 1987 (3 of 1988)

The Constitution of India, 1950

The Dowry Prohibition Act, 1961 (28 of 1961) (Amended in 1986)

The Employees' State Insurance Act,1948

The Equal Remuneration Act, 1976

The Factories Act, 1948

The Family Courts Act, 1984

The Foreign Marriage Act, 1969 (33 of 1969)

The Guardians and Wards Act,1890

The Hindu Adoptions & Maintenance Act, 1956

The Hindu Marriage Act, 1955 (28 of 1989)

The Hindu Minority & Guardianship Act, 1956

The Hindu Succession Act, 1956

The Immoral Traffic (Prevention) Act, 1956

The Indecent Representation of Women (Prohibition) Act, 1986

The Indian Christian Marriage Act, 1872 (15 of 1872)

The Indian Divorce Act, 1969 (4 of 1969)

The Indian Evidence Act, 1872

The Indian Penal Code,1860

The Inter-State Migrant Workmen (Regulation of Employment and Conditions of Service) Act, 1979

The Married Women's Property Act, 1874 (3 of 1874)

The Maternity Benefit Act, 1961 (53 of 1961)

The Medical Termination of Pregnancy Act, 1971 (34 of 1971)

The Mines Act 1952

The Minimum Wages Act, 1948

The Minimum Wages Act, 1950

The Muslim Personal Law (Shariat) Application Act, 1937

The Muslim women Protection of Rights on Dowry Act 1986

The Payments of Wages (Procedure) Act, 1937

The Payments of Wages Act, 1936

The Plantation Labour Act, 1951 (amended by Acts Nos. 42 of 1953, 34 of 1960, 53 of1961, 58 of 1981and 61 of 1986)

The Pre-Natal Diagnostic Techniques (Regulation and Prevention of misuse) Act 1994

The Protection of Civil Rights Act 1955

The Protection of Human Rights Act, 1993 [As amended by the Protection of Human Rights (Amendment) Act, 2006–No. 43 of 2006]

The Sexual Harassment of Women at Workplace (PREVENTION, PROHIBITION and REDRESSAL) Act, 2013

The Special Marriage Act, 1954

The Trade Unions Act 1926

The Workmen's Compensation Act, 1923

WEBSITES :

Gender Equality and Justice Programming: Equitable Access to Justice for Women

http://altlawforum.org/resources/sexwork

http://debaraticyberspace.blogspot.in

http://equalbeforethelaw.org/library/doing-justice-how-informal-justice-systems-can-contribute

http://lawmatters.in/wp-content/uploads/2010/03/dv.pdf

http://ncw.nic.in.

http://nhrc.nic.in

http://perry4law.co.in/cc.html

http://timesofindia.indiatimes.com/topic/Cyber-Crimes-Bureau

http://www.csi-india.org/c/document_library/get_file?uuid=70d4bc4a-8548-4375-adb6-15654dc9d068&groupId=10157

http://www.deccanchronicle.com/130123/news-crime/article/crime-file-cyber-crime-case-against-professors

http://www.domesticviolence.in/

http://www.du.ac.in/fileadmin/DU/Academics/course_material/hrge_10.pdf

http://www.education.qld.gov.au/actsmartbesafe/violence/sexual.html.

http://www.elixirpublishers.com/articles/1351168842_47%20(2012)%208891-8895.pdf

http://www.goforthelaw.com/index.php/browsearticles/loadarticleview/214.html

http://www.helpline la http://

http://www.helplinelaw.com/docs/violence.php

http://www.hindustantimes.com/india-news/mumbai/cyber-crime-against-women-on-the-rise/article1-571518.aspx

http://www.indiankanoon.com

http://www.indiastudychannel.com/resources/149173-Women-Indian-Mass-Media-How-media-represents.aspx

http://www.indiatvnews.com/crime/news/five-spine-chilling-cases-of-honour-killings-in-india-3601.html?

http://www.lawyerscollective.org/womens-rights-initiative/cedaw.html

http://www.legalserviceindia.com/article/1263-Domestic-violence-in-Marriage.html.

http://www.legalserviceindia.com/articles/dmt.htm

http://www.legalservicesindia.com/article/article/crime-against-women-&-its-impact-on-them-540-1.html

http://www.legalservicesindia.com/article/print.php?art_id=415

http://www.manupatra.com

http://www.mightylaws.in/803/improper-portrayal-women-media

http://www.ndtv.com/article/cheat-sheet/recommendations-of-the-justice-verma-committee-10-point-cheat-sheet-321734

http://www.ndtv.com/article/india/new-anti-rape-legislation-criminal-law-amendment-ordinance-2013-326240

http://www.peoples-health.com/finantialabuse.html.

http://www.thehindu.com/news/national/stringent-antirape-laws-get-presidents-nod/article4576695.ece

http://www.thehindu.com/news/resources/full-text-of-justice-vermas-report-pdf/article4339457.ece

http://www.tmu.ac.in/gallery/viewpointsdcip2013/pdf/track4/t-403.pdf

http://www.un.org/rights/dpi1772e.htm

http://www.undp.org/content/undp/en/home/librarypage/womens-empowerment/gender-equality-and-justice-programming-equitable-access-to-justice-for-women1/

http://www.womensaid.org.uk/domestic-violence-articles.asp?section=00010001002200410001&itemid=1274

http://www.yfn.co.in/stop-women-abuse

www.un.org/millenniumgoalsw.com/docs

http://ibnlive.in.com/news/government-releases-national-cyber-security-policy-2013/403473-11.html?utm_source=ref_article

http://www.ilo.org/ipec/facts/lang--en/index.htm

http://articles.timesofindia.indiatimes.com/2012-08-26/india/33401779_1_child-labour-labour-department-aditi-mehta

http://vegaselias.hubpages.com/hub/CHILD-LABOR-IN-INDIA-AND-ITS-CAUSES

http://honourcrimes.wordpress.com/

http://lawcommissionofindia.nic.in/reports/report242.pdf

http://heinonline.org/HOL/Page?handle=hein.journals/nilq55&div=12&g_sent=1&collection=journals#86 1

http://www.jstor.org/stable/4017752

INTERNATIONAL DOCUMENTS

The United Nations Special Rapporteur on the right of everyone to the enjoyment of the highest attainable standard of physical and mental health (2006).

International Covenant on Economic, Social and Cultural Rights, adopted 16 Dec. 1966, 993 U.N.T.S. 3 (entered into force 3 Jan. 1976), art. 12(1), G.A. Res. 2200 (XXI), 21 U.N. GAOR, Supp. (No. 16), at 49, U.N. Doc. A/6316 (1966)

Applying Rights Rhetoric to Social and Economic Claims, Session I of the

Dr. Sushma Sharma

Economic and Social Rights and the Right to Health Conference (Sept. 1993), in ECONOMIC AND SOCIAL RIGHTS AND THE RIGHT TO HEALT

Article 1 of the Universal Declaration of Human Rights proclaims: "All human beings are born free and equal in dignity and rights. They are endowed with reason and conscience and should act towards one another in a spirit of brotherhood."

Universal Declaration of Human Rights, adopted 10 Dec. 1948, G.A. Res. 217A (11), 3 U.N. GAOR (Resolutions, part 1) at 71, U.N. Doc. A/810 (1948), reprinted in 43 AM. J. INT'L L. SuPP. 127, 128 (1949) [hereinafter UDHR

Convention on the Elimination of All Forms of Discrimination Against Women, adopted 18 Dec. 1979, Arts. 10, 12, G.A. Res. 34/180, U.N. GAOR Supp. (No. 46), U.N. Doc. A/34/36 (1978

WORLD HEALTH ORGANIZATION, PRIMARY HEALTH CARE: REPORT OF THE INTERNATIONAL CONFERENCE ON PRIMARY HEALTH CARE (1978)

Committee on Economic, Social and Cultural Rights, Report on the Fifth Session (26 November-14 December 1990), U.N. ESCOR, Annex III, Supp. No. 3, at 86, U.N. Doc. E/1991/23 (1991), E/C.12/1990/8 (1990) (General Comment No. 3, The Nature of State Parties' Obligation

Vienna Declaration and Programme of Action (A/CONF.157/23), adopted by the World Conference on Human Rights, held in Vienna, 14–25 June

1993

World Health Organization, Water, sanitation and hygiene: Quantifying the health impact at national and local levels in countries with incomplete water supply and sanitation coverage, Environmental Burden of Disease Series, No. 15 (Geneva, 2007).

Defining the Right to Adequate Health, Session II of the Harvard Symposium, in ECONOMIC AND SOCIAL RIGHTS AND THE RIGHT TO HEALTH, supra note 5, at 17 (remarks of Jonathan Mann)

Defining the Right to Adequate Health, Session II of the Harvard Symposium, in ECONOMIC AND SOCIAL RIGHTS AND THE RIGHT TO HEALTH, supra note 5, at 34 (remarks of Martha Nussbaum

Declaration of Alma-Ata, International Conference on Primary Health Care, Alma-Ata, USSR, September 1978.

General Assembly resolution S-26/2 of 27 July 2001

Office of the United Nations High Commissioner for Human Rights, World Health Organization, The Right to Health, Fact Sheet No. 31

Report of the International Conference on Population and Development, Cairo, 5–13 September 1994 (United Nations publication, Sales N° E.95.XIII.18).

Beijing Declaration and Platform for Action, Report of the Fourth World Conference on Women, Beijing, 4–15 September 1995 (United Nations publication, Sales N° E.96.IV.13), chap. I, resolution 1.

ABOUT THE AUTHOR

Dr. Sushma Sharma was born on 30th of May 1973 in Bhopal, Madhya Pradesh, she obtained her B.Sc., LL.M. and Ph.D. degrees from Barkatullah University, Bhopal, and also secured positions in the list of merit. She began her career in law in 2001 with the Madhya Pradesh Human Rights Commission where she worked as a Research Officer for a period of about four years. She started teaching law in The National law Institute University, Bhopal in the year 2006 where she was appointed as an Assistant Professor of Administrative Justice System and since then she is working there. She has authored a book, Administrative Justice System in India. Her areas of special interest include administrative law, human rights and constitutional law.

END-NOTES

[i] Article 1 of the said Convention reads as follows:

For the purposes of the present Convention, the term "discrimination against women " shall mean any distinction, exclusion or restriction made on the basis of sex which has the effect or purpose of impairing or nullifying the recognition, enjoyment or exercise by women, irrespective of their marital status, on a basis of equality of men and women, of human rights and fundamental freedoms in the political, economic, social, cultural, civil or any other field.

Sub Article (1) of Article 11 of the Convention, which has its own signification, is as follows:

1. States Parties shall take all appropriate measures to eliminate discrimination against women in the field of employment in order to ensure, on a basis of equality of men and women , the same rights, in particular:

[ii] (a) The right to work as an inalienable right of all human beings;

(b) The right to the same employment opportunities, including the application of the same criteria for selection in matters of employment;

(c) The right to free choice of profession and employment, the right to promotion, job security and all benefits and conditions of service and the right to receive vocational training and retraining, including apprenticeships, advanced vocational training and recurrent training;

(d) The right to equal remuneration, including benefits, and to equal treatment in respect of work of equal value, as well as equality of treatment in the evaluation of the quality of work;

(e) The right to social security, particularly in cases of retirement, unemployment, sickness, invalidity and old age and other incapacity to work, as well as the right to paid leave;

(f) The right to protection of health and to safety in working conditions, including the safeguarding of the function of reproduction.

[iii] (1980) 3 SCC 625
[iv] (2012) 6 SCC 1
[v] (1996) 3 SCC 545,
[vi] (1996) 5 SCC 125
[vii] (SCC) p. 148, para 28
[viii] (2013) 4 SCC 1
(1992) 1 SCC 286 [ix]
[x] (1986) 1 SCR 743
[xi] (1987) 2 SCC 469
[xii] AIR 1997 SC 3011
[xiii] (2003) SCC 224
[xiv] (2015)1SCC 192
[xv] Domestic Violence in Marriage: in the light of theories of Feminist Jurisprudence, http://www.legalserviceindia.com/article/1263-Domestic-Violence-in-Marriage.html

[xvi] Little Oxford English Dictionary, 6th impression 2007, Oxford university press, p.785.
[xvii] Nandita Saikia, Domestic Violence Handbook http://lawmatters.in/wp-content/uploads
[xviii] Sri Krishna Kumar, Crime Against Women & its Impact on Them http://www.legalservicesindia.com/article/article/crime-against-women-&-its-impact-on-them-540-1.html
[xix] http://www.lawyerscollective.org/womens-rights-initiative/cedaw.html
[xx] http://www.un.org/rights/dpi1772e.htm
[xxi] Domestic violence , http://www.domesticviolence.in/

[xxii] Domestic violence ,http://www.domesticviolence.in/

[xxiii] Domestic Violence in Marriage: in the light of

theories of Feminist Jurisprudence,

http://www.legalserviceindia.com/article/l263-Domestic-Violence-in-Marriage.html)

xxiv Domestic violence in India, http://www.helplinelaw.com/docs/violence.php

xxv Oxford pocket English dictionary,6th impression2007, Oxford university press,p.513.

xxvi What are the effects of domestic abuse on women?, Women's Aid Federation of England. http://www.womensaid.org.uk/domestic-violence-articles

xxvii *What is financial or economical abuse*, http://www.peoples-health.com/financial_abuse.htm

xxviii Sexual abuse(http://education.qld.gov.au/actsmartbesafe/violence/sexual.html)

xxix Bare act, protection of women from domestic violence act(http://www.helplinelaw.com/docs/)

xxx Verbal abuse in relationship (http://www.verbalabuse.com/3.shtml)

xxxi Bare act, protection of women from domestic violence act(http://www.helplinelaw.com/docs/)

xxxii Harini Sudersan, The Domestic Violence Act : Constitutional Perspective http://www.legalserviceindia.com/articles/dmt.htm

xxxiii Padmalaya Mahapatra, Domestic violence: issue of violation of human rights of women, Madhya Pradesh Journal of Social Sciences 2008

xxxiv Raj Bahadur Singh Verma, Towards Empowering Indian Women: Mapping Specifics of Tasks in Crucial Sectors, 2007 Serials Publications, New Delhi

xxxv Supra n. 5

xxxvi Dorothy Q. Thomas, Domestic Violence as a Human Rights Issue, Human Rights Quarterly, Vol. 15, No. 1 (Feb., 1993), pp. 36-62

xxxvii http://wji-hrln.blogspot.in/2010/03/general-recommendation-no-19-violence.html

xxxviii http://wji-hrln.blogspot.in/2010/03/vienna-declaration-and-programme-of.html

xxxix Mary Scaria, Woman: An Endangered Species, 2006 Media House, Delhi

xl Section 4 of The Protection of Women from Domestic Violence Act, 2005

xli Section 5 of The Protection of Women from Domestic Violence Act, 2005

[xlii] Section 6 and 7 of The Protection of Women from Domestic Violence Act, 2005
[xliii] http://streeshakthi.hpage.co.in/domestic-violence-act_32117850.html
[xliv] http://sahodar.org/domesticvoilanceact.htm
[xlv] http://www.rediff.com/news/special/spec/20061101.htm
[xlvi] Supra n. 22
[xlvii] AIR 1978 SC 597
[xlviii] 1997 (11) SCC 123
[xlix] AIR 1996 SC 1051
[l] 2001 (1) CAL 535
[li] 2010 ILR (4) Delhi 383
[lii] *Bengal Immunity Co. Vs. State of Bihar,* AIR 1955 SC 661
[liii] State of A.P. Vs. Nallmillin Rami Reddi, AIR 2001 SC 3616
[liv] 2008 (2) MLJ 389.
[lv] 2011(1)KLT 609(SC)
[lvi] Judgement on 31 January, 2013, Cr. Revision No.871 of 2012
[lvii] AIR 2013 SC 329
[lviii] (2010) 158 PLR 1
[lix] 2012 KHC 2598
[lx] Freedman, Lynn P.; Stephen L. Isaacs (Jan. - Feb. 1993). "Human Rights and Reproductive Choice". Studies in Family Planning (Studies in Family Planning, Vol. 24, No. 1) 24 (1): 18–30. doi:10.2307/2939211. JSTOR 2939211. PMID 8475521.
[lxi] Supra note 1.
[lxii] Center for Reproductive Rights, International Legal Program, Establishing International Reproductive Rights Norms: Theory for Change, US CONG. REC. 108th CONG. 1 Sess. E2534 E2547 (Rep. Smith) (Dec. 8, 2003)

[lxiii] Knudsen, Lara (2006). Reproductive Rights in a Global Context. Vanderbilt University Press. pp. 7. ISBN 0-8265-1528-2, 9780826515285. http://books.google.com/?id=b3thCcdyScsC&dq=reproductive+rights.

[lxiv] United Nations, Report of the Fourth International Conference on Population and Development, Cario, 5 - 13 September 1994

[lxv] http://india.mapsofindia.com/india-forum/womens-in-india.html

[lxvi] http://indiacurrentaffairs.org/women-empowerment-equal-rights-equal-

opportunities-smt-anita-patnaik/

[lxvii] On 18th of December 2012 Supreme Court gave capital punishmet to three people in a case of hour killing. On 7th of November 2010 , Puja and her lover who were inhabitants of a village Noorpur Sethan, were murdered In village Kotwal, Firozpur, Punjab. The girl and her lover Rakesh were called saying that their wedding will be arranged and were murdered by Puja's mother, her maternal uncle and one other person.(Reported on page 15, Dainik Bhaskar,Wed. 19 Dec 1012.)
[lxviii] 1979 AIR 1868; 1979 SCC (4) 260
[lxix] 1997 (6) SCC 241
[lxx] AIR 1978 SC 12; 1977 (4) SCC 334]
[lxxi] AIR 1981 SC 1829; 1981 (4) SCC 335
[lxxii] 1992 AIR 392: 1992 SCC (1) 286
[lxxiii] 2008 III LLJ 58 (SC)
[lxxiv] Encyclopedia of Human Rights. Vol.4

[lxxv] Center of Excellence in Disaster Management & Humanitarian Assistance (COEDMHA), 2 February 2006, Indian police says 1,086 people killed in 2005 in separatist violence in Indian controlled Kashmir (ICK) 26.03.2013

[lxxvi] The Observer Research Foundation, 3 September 2003, Recommendations made at the Conference on Kashmiri Pandits 2-3 September 2003. 26.03.2013

[lxxvii] Amnesty International (AI), 2 December 2003, India - Open Letter to the Chief Minister of Jammu and Kashmir on the failed promises of the Common Minimum Program, AI INDEX: ASA 20/033/2003; Center of Excellence in Disaster Management & Humanitarian Assistance (COEDMHA, "Report says 121 people disappeared since November 2002; 400 people killed this year in Indian-controlled Kashmir (ICK)".

[lxxviii] Center of Excellence in Disaster Management & Humanitarian Assistance (COEDMHA), 2 April 2004,"Election campaigners in India's restive northeast threatened by rebels".

[lxxix] Bhaumik, Subir, March 2000, Internal Displacement in Northeast India: Challenges Ahead, in Refugee Watch of the South Asia Forum For Human

Rights, No.9, p.22-24 26.03.2013

[lxxx] BBC News, 9 December 2005, Assam's paths of violence.
[lxxxi] The Hindu, 2 December 2003, "Relief package for violence-hit in State"; Frontline, 6 December 2003, "Outrage in Assam" Vol. 20, Issue

[lxxxii] Center of Excellence in Disaster Management & Humanitarian Assistance (COEDMHA), 19 April 2005, Rebels in India's northeastern Assam state extend ceasefire with Indian government;1 killed, 8 injured in bomb blast in Manipur

[lxxxiii] BBC News, 9 December 2005, Assam's paths of violence.
[lxxxiv] Center of Excellence in Disaster Management & Humanitarian Assistance (COEDMHA), 28 December 2005, Fresh tribal violence breaks out in India's northeastern Assam state; Médecins Sans Frontières, 2006, Voices from the Field: "Houses and whole villages have been burned"

[lxxxv] Sangai Express, 21 January 2006, Govt assures relief to Displaced villagers

[lxxxvi] Deccan Herald, 22 May 2005, Displaced Tripura villagers demand rehabilitation Deccan Herald, 20 March 2004, "Terror-struck Tripura families seek safety in Bangladesh"

[lxxxvii] Institute of Peace and Conflict Studies (IPCS), 19 September 2003, Refugees and Security: The Cases of Arunachal Pradesh and Mizoram.

[lxxxviii] Institute of Peace and Conflict Studies (IPCS), 17 January 2004, Case for an IDP Database in India's Northeast.

[lxxxix] Haldar, Chiranjib, March 2007, The Nepali Influx in Northeast India

[xc] Asian Centre for Human Rights (ACHR), 21 September 2005, Naxalism and civil wars of India; Frontline, 15 July 2005, A naxalite corridor.

[xci] Asian Centre for Human Rights (ACHR), 21 September 2005, Naxalism and civil wars of India; Frontline, 15 July 2005, A naxalite corridor. 27.03.2013

[xcii] South Asia Analysis Group (SAAG), 13 June 2005, Messing up with Naxalites, by Col R. Hariharan.
[xciii] People's Union for Civil Liberties (PUCL), 2 December 2005, Fact-finding report on the Salwa Judum, Dantewara District.

[xciv] http://www.uni-bielefeld.de/tdrc/ag_comcad/downloads/workingpaper_103_negi_ganguly.pdf 03.04.2013

[xcv] AIR 1992,2 SCC 202

[xcvi] AIR 1986; Supp. SCC 578

[xcvii] Article 1 of the said Convention reads as follows:

For the purposes of the present Convention, the term "discrimination against women " shall mean any distinction, exclusion or restriction made on the basis of sex which has the effect or purpose of impairing or nullifying the recognition, enjoyment or exercise by women, irrespective of their marital status, on a basis of equality of men and women, of human rights and fundamental freedoms in the political, economic, social, cultural, civil or any other field.

Sub Article (1) of Article 11 of the Convention, which has its own signification, is as follows:

1. States Parties shall take all appropriate measures to eliminate discrimination against women in the field of employment in order to ensure, on a basis of equality of men and women , the same rights, in particular:

[xcviii] (a) The right to work as an inalienable right of all human beings;

(b) The right to the same employment opportunities, including the application of the same criteria for selection in matters of employment;

(c) The right to free choice of profession and employment, the right to promotion, job security and all benefits and conditions of service and the right to receive vocational training and retraining, including apprenticeships, advanced vocational training and recurrent training;

(d) The right to equal remuneration, including benefits, and to equal treatment in respect of work of equal value, as well as equality of treatment in the evaluation of the quality of work;

(e) The right to social security, particularly in cases of retirement, unemployment, sickness, invalidity and old age and other incapacity to work, as well as the right to paid leave;

(f) The right to protection of health and to safety in working conditions, including the safeguarding of the function of reproduction.

[xcix] (1992)1 S.C.C.289
[c] 1996 AIR 309, 1995 SCC (6) 194
[ci] (1996) 3 SCC 545,
[cii] AIR 1997 SC 3011

[ciii] A.I.R.1999 S.C.625
[civ] en.wikipedia.org/wiki/Criminal_Law_(Amendment)_Act,_2013
[cv] Ahmad, N. (September 2011). "Acid attacks on women: An appraisal of the Indian legal response". Asia Pacific Journal On Human Rights And The Law 12 (2): 55–72. 3 "I have lost everything", The Times of India, Benet Coleman&co. Nov.21, 2012 4 Sec. 354, Indian Penal Code
[cvi] *1994 SCR (1) 37*
[cvii] *17 (1980) DLT 404*
[cviii] *1979 AIR 185*
[cix] *2000 CRI. L.J. 1473*
[cx] *1997 IVAD Delhi 646*
[cxi] *1997 6 SCC 241*
[cxii] *1996 AIR 922*
[cxiii] Sharma, Divya : (2009) "Honour Killings : A Slaur on Humanity". Lawyers update, Sept., at 46
[cxiv] Lawz Bureau : „Analysis on Honour Killing; Lawz Media (P) Ltd., New

Delhi, Vol. 10, No. 8, Issue 108, pp 10-13.

cxv Originally it is a Baluch and Pashtun tribal custom, where honour killings are founded in the twin concepts of honour and commoditization of women. Women are married off for a bride price paid to the father. This was basically a baloch and pashlun tribal custom, honour killings are not only reported in Baluchistan, NWFP and Upper Sindh which has a Baloch influx, but in Punjab province as well. If this commodity is damaged toe proprietor, the father or husband has a right to compensation. Besides this, many countries are very notorious for honour killing, such as Arab or Muslim countries like Pakistan, Turkey, Iraq, Jordan and Palestine. In India many such murders are committed by Hindus and Sikhs. For some Hindus, an honour killing may be motivated by a woman marrying across the cast boundaries.

cxvi (Hassan 1995)

cxvii (Oxford Dictionary of Law Enforcement 2007)

cxviii (Amnesty International 1999)

cxix ibid

cxx *Honour killings: New law needed,* (Nov. 18th, 2010)

cxxi Article 3 of the Universal Declaration of Human Rights. 1948.

cxxii Ibid., Article 16.

cxxiii Prem Chowdhry. —Contentious Marriages, Eloping Couples: Gender, Caste and Patriarchy in Northern India‖.2007.

cxxiv Sharma, Dr. Sobharam (2011) "Honour Killings in India: Need for Deterrent Action", LawZ, LawZ Media (P) Ltd., New Delhi, Vol.II, No.2, Issue 114, Pp.15-18.

cxxv Choudhury, D.R.: (2011) "Khaps Shouldn't be allowed, to have their Way" The Tribune. December 20, 2011 posted by NNLRJ India.

cxxvi See Editorial remarks "Half Steps against Honour Crimes", EPW, February 18,2012 at 7

cxxvii Sangwan, Fagmati : (2010) "Khap Panchayat : Signs of desperation ?" The Hindu, Visakhapatnam, May 8, at 10.

cxxviii The Ministry of Home Affairs, Government of India, vide its D.O. No. 12/24/2009 – Judl. Cell dated July 8, 2010.

cxxix The home Department, Government of Haryana, vide its letter No. 14/26/2010-31(C) dated 8.9.2010 to the centre and see also The Chief Minister of Haryana State vide its D.O. No. CMH-2010 PSC pi/3453 dt. 30.9.2013. The above mentioned letter states that there is no need for fresh legislation to deal with the problem rather it is a sinister and motivational work done by megalomanial media. 14

cxxx Section 2(1), The Prohibition of Unlawful Assembly (Interference with the Freedom of matrimonial Alliances) Bill, 2011.

cxxxi Ibid, Explanation appended to Sec. 2(1).

cxxxii Ibid, Sec. 8.

cxxxiii Ibid. Sec. 4.

cxxxiv Ibid. Sec. 12
cxxxv Ibid. Sec. 9
cxxxvi Manoj-Babli case. (n.d.). Retrieved November 27, 2013, from http://www.dailyindia.com/show/429294.php
cxxxvii Sangwan, Fagmati : (2010) "Khap Panchayat : Signs of desperation ?" The Hindu, Visakhapatnam, May 8, at 10.
cxxxviii AIR 2006 S.C. 2522.
cxxxix Ibid at 2524 (Para 14).
cxl (2011)6 SCC 405
cxli Ibid. (Para 12).
cxlii AIR 2010 SC 3071
cxliii Bhagwan Das vs. State (Nct) of Delhi, Criminal Appeal No. 1117 of 2011. Retrieved December 3, 2013, from http://www.indiankanoon.org/doc/1422914/
cxliv http://www.lawteacher.net
cxlv https://en.wikipedia.org/wiki/Child
cxlvi http://www.lawteacher.net

cxlvii http://unicef.in/Whatwedo/30/Child-Marriage#sthash.Sv2xtIU2.dpuf

cxlviii Air 2001 Delhi 212
cxlix [1982 II LLJ 454 SC (1982) 3 SCC 235]
cl [1984 3 SCC 161]

cli W.P. (c)9767/2009

clii AIR 1997 SC 699
cliii -1998 (4) SCC 270
cliv Atharva Veda (5.30.6)

clv Definition of an Environmental Right in a Human Rights Context *Philippe Cullet*, http://www.ielrc.org/content/a9502.pdf
clvi HeinOnline -- 13 Neth. Q. Hum. Rts. 25 1995 *NQHIR 1 / 1995*

clvii HeinOnline -- 13 Neth. Q. Hum. Rts. 26 1995
Cullet / Definition of an Environmental Right in a Human Rights Context

clviii AIR 1980 SC 1622
clix (1987) 2 SCC 295

clx 1986 (2) SCC 176 (at page 202)
clxi W.P. no .13029 of 1985
clxii 989 AIR 594 1989 SCC Supl. (1) 537 JT 1988 (4) 710 1988 SCALE (2)1574
clxiii (1991) 1 SCC 598
clxiv (1995) 2 SCC 577
clxv 1996 (5) SCC 647
clxvi 1996 (2) 196
clxvii 1999(2) SCC 718
clxviii AIR2004SC4016, 2004(3)SCALE396, (2004)12SCC118
clxix Preamble to the Constitution of the World Health Organization as adopted by the International Health Conference, New York, 19–22 June 1946; signed on 22 July 1947 by the representatives of 61 States (Official Records of the World Health Organization, no. 2, p. 100); and entered into force on 7 April 1948
clxx Constitution of World Health Organization, The Constitution was adopted by the International Health Conference held in New York from 19 June to 22 July 1946, signed on 22 July 1946.

clxxi Justice K.G. Balakrishnan, Chief Justice of India, Address at the National seminar on the 'Human right to health' Organized by the Madhya Pradesh State Human Rights Commission (At Bhopal) - September 14, 2008

clxxiii The origins of WHO go back to the various international health conferences held in the nineteenth century, the first in Paris in 1851. The Pan American Health Organization (PAHO, founded in Washington in 1902), the *Office International d'Hygiène Publique* (founded in Rome in 1907), and the International Labour Organization (1919), are its immediate forerunners.

clxxiv Constitution of the World Health Organization, *Basic Documents*, Official Document No. 240 (Washington, 1991). The Constitution of WHO was adopted at the International Health Conference held in 1946 in

New York, where it was signed by the representatives of sixty-one states (hereafter coted as WHO Constitution).

clxxv WHO, Declaration of Alma-Ata, International Conference on Primary Health Care, Alma-Ata, USSR, 6-12 September 1978.
clxxvi The 1965 International Convention on the Elimination of All Forms of Racial Discrimination: art. 5 (e) (iv) 2. The steps to be taken by the States Parties to the present Covenant to achieve the full realization of this right shall include those necessary for:

> (a) The provision for the reduction of the stillbirth rate and of infant mortality and for the healthy development of the child;

> (b) The improvement of all aspects of environmental and industrial hygiene;

> (c) The prevention, treatment and control of epidemic, endemic, occupational and other diseases;

> (d) The creation of conditions which would assure to all medical service and medical attention in the event of sickness.

Subsequent international and regional human rights instruments address the right to health in various ways. Some are of general application while others address the human rights of specific groups, such as women or children.

clxxvii **Art. 12**

1. The States Parties to the present Covenant recognize the right of everyone to the enjoyment of the highest attainable standard of physical and mental health.

clxxviii (1989) 4 SCC 286

clxxix 1996 SCC (4) 37, JT 1996 (6) 43
clxxx 1984 (3) SCC 161
clxxxi 1989 AIR 1570, 1989 SCR (3) 241
clxxxii AIR 1996 SC 929

clxxxiii 1998 (6) SCALE 230; 1998 (8) SCC 296; JT 1998 (7) SC. 626).
clxxxiv Ex-Chief Justice of India Adarsh Sen Anand November 1999: http://www.hrln.org/hrln/prisoners-rights.html#ixzz3xaecSMKF

clxxxv V.R.Krishna Iyer, "National Prison Policy Constitutional Perspective and Pragmatic Parameters."

Sir.AlladiKrishnaiSwamii Iyer, Endowment Lecture (1981), p.26

clxxxvi https://en.wikipedia.org/wiki/Prisoners%E2%80%99_rights_in_international_law

clxxxvii Adopted by the First United Nations Congress on the Prevention of Crime and the Treatment of Offenders, held at Geneva in 1955, and approved by the Economic and Social Council by its resolutions 663 C (XXIV) of 31 July 1957 and 2076 (LXII) of 13 May 1977

clxxxviii http://www.hrln.org/hrln/prisoners-rights.html#ixzz3xaevfW8P

clxxxix [1979] 1 SCR 192
cxc 1980 AIR 1579, 1980 SCR (2) 557
cxci 1966 AIR 424, 1966 SCR (1) 702

cxcii (1978) 4 SCC 409
cxciii 1993 Cri LJ 3242
cxciv 1978 (4) SCC 104; AIR 1978 SC 1514
cxcv 1981 (1) SCC 608, AIR 1981 SC 746
cxcvi AIR 1979 SC 1369 : 1979 Cri LJ 1052.
cxcvii 2009 (7) SCC 104
cxcviii 1980 (3) SCC 526, AIR 1980 SC 1535
cxcix *AIR1997SC1739, 1997CriLJ1508, 1997(1)SCALE95, (1997)2SCC642*
cc MANU/SC/0084/1980 : 1980CriLJ930
cci MANU/SC/0562/1993 : (1993)4SCC204
ccii 1996 AIR 1619, 1996 SCC (4) 33
cciii *Fertilizer Corpn. Kamgar Union (Regd.) v. Union of India, S.P. Gupta, People's Union for Democratic Rights, D.C. Wadhwa (Dr) v. State of Bihar and BALCO Employees' Union (Regd.) v. Union of India.*
cciv (2002) 2 SCC 333, Para Nos. 78 and 80

[ccv] AIR 1984 SC 802.

[ccvi] AIR 1984 SC 177.

[ccvii] AIR 1985 SC 652

[ccviii] AIR1987SC 355.

[ccix] 1997 (6) SCC 241